FRENCH CHARCUTERIE AT HOME

TERRINES RILLETTES SAUCISSES & PÂTÉS EN CROÛTE

To Catherine, Cécile, and Thomas,
who share our lives and our passions

Gilles & Nicolas Verot

FRENCH CHARCUTERIE AT HOME

TERRINES RILLETTES SAUCISSES & PÂTÉS EN CROÛTE

PHOTOGRAPHED BY DAVID JAPY AND ILLUSTRATED BY ÉLIANE CHEUNG

tra.publishing

FOREWORD

Gilles is a third-generation Master Charcuterie who has won numerous accolades including the world champion of Pâté en Croûte. His knowledge of this culinary art, which dates back to the 15 th century, is one of the greatest, and he and his son continue to build on the historical foundation to move charcuterie forward.

I first met Gilles in 2005 and knew I had to work with him after our first meeting. I wanted to introduce the traditions of charcuterie to New York and he was the perfect person to help me accomplish this. Like me, Gilles has an appreciation for using seasonal and local ingredients and is inspired by what is around him. We worked together to develop a program in New York (beginning with my restaurant Bar Boulud) that was rooted in French tradition, technique and used the best local ingredients for all the pâtés, terrines, rillettes, ham, and sausages. We developed many recipes together and adapted them for our menus in New York.

Gilles is now passing the art of charcuterie to his son, Nicolas, and together they continue to be very creative and push the boundaries of this inspiring tradition in this book. The recipes teach proper technique and have a strong foundation for building any terrine, pâté, sausage or rilletes, and go beyond to elevate taste and texture with interesting seasonings and new flavors.

This book focuses on seasonality, highlights the true art of charcuterie and introduces soulful French cooking into your home. I am so enthusiastic for this edition in English. It will expand your passion for cooking with the Verot Family.

DANIEL BOULUD

MAKING CHARCUTERIE AT HOME IS EASY—
WE WROTE THIS BOOK TO SHOW YOU!

We are father-and-son charcuterie makers working side by side in our family business, Maison Verot, which began its journey in 1930. Together with our team, we strive each day to produce high-quality products that are healthy and environmentally friendly.

This book gathers traditional charcuterie recipes, reminiscent of the French concept of terroir (which encompasses the effects of the soil, topography, and environment on the food grown), alongside modern creations that are lighter and more vegetable-focused. You will find classics like country pâté and innovative dishes such as vegetable rillettes.

We've created every recipe under typical home kitchen conditions, often using just a knife, a mixing bowl, a mold, and an oven. For this reason, some traditional charcuterie staples, like blood sausage, ham, or salami, are absent from the book. We've focused on recipes that can be easily replicated at home.

We're passionate about sharing our expertise and making Maison Verot's style accessible for everyday cooking. We developed these recipes with three constraints: readily available ingredients, the exclusive use of basic kitchen tools, and minimal technical jargon.

So, this book is for everyone! Whether you're a novice or an experienced cook, you'll find both delight and a challenge here.

GILLES AND NICOLAS VEROT

CONTENTS

BASIC UTENSILS

◆ ◆ ◆

Nearly all the recipes in this book can be executed with just a knife, a mixing bowl, and a mold, but other basic tools will quickly prove essential for anyone interested in making charcuterie.

PARING KNIFE

It's the smallest of knives, perfect for slicing fruits and vegetables.

CHEF'S KNIFE

Highly versatile, it's used for cutting and chopping meat or any other large ingredient.

PEELER

Ideal for peeling the majority of fruits and vegetables, especially those with thin skins.

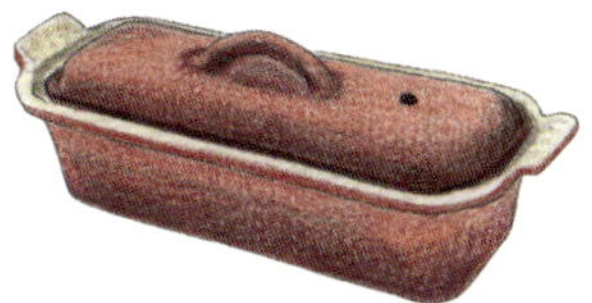

TERRINE

A traditional container for many charcuterie specialties.

LOAF PAN

If you don't have a terrine, a loaf pan can be used as a substitute.

SKILLET

Helpful for sautéing or searing some meats and other ingredients.

SAUCEPAN

Crucial for cooking rillettes and many pressed dishes.

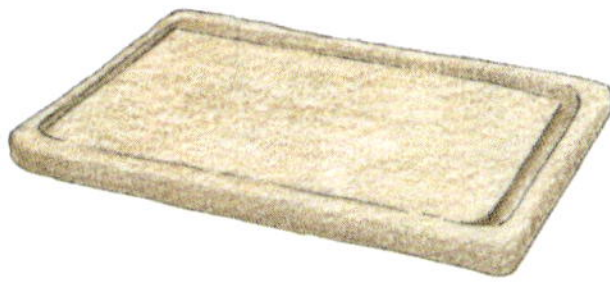

CUTTING BOARD

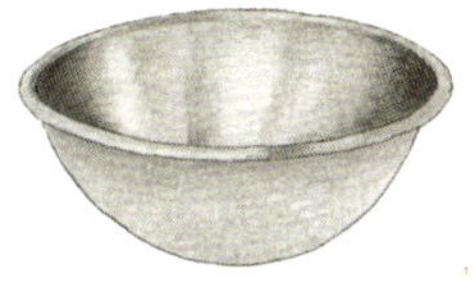

MIXING BOWL OR CHEF'S BOWL

Choose one that's two to three times larger than the volume of ingredients.

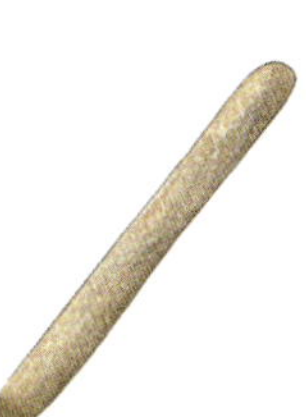

ROLLING PIN

SPATULA

PASTRY BRUSH

KITCHEN SCALE

GOING FURTHER

◆ ◆ ◆

If you aspire to take your charcuterie skills to the next level,
it may be worthwhile to invest in specialized tools,
such as specific types of knives, a grinder, and a sausage stuffer.

BONING KNIFE

This is a medium-sized knife with a very fine tip, perfect for deboning and trimming meats.

PÂTÉ EN CROÛTE KNIFE

Featuring teeth to cut through pastry, its blade is thinner than that of a bread knife, ensuring the slices remain intact.

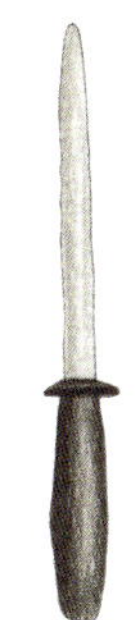

SHARPENING STEEL

Used for regularly honing knives to ensure they cut properly and last longer.

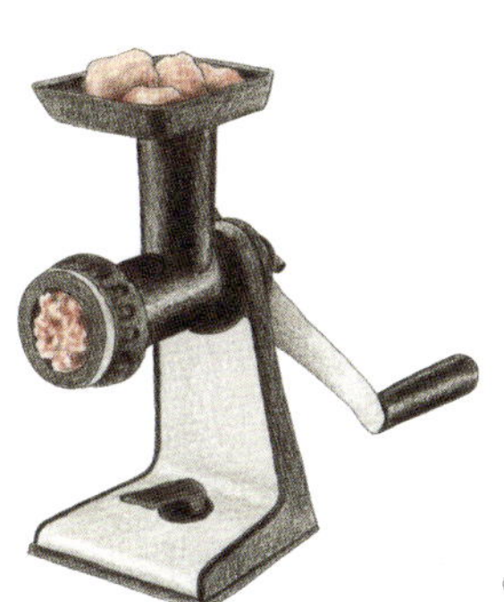

MEAT GRINDER

Not to be confused with a blender, it grinds meats to various degrees of fineness.

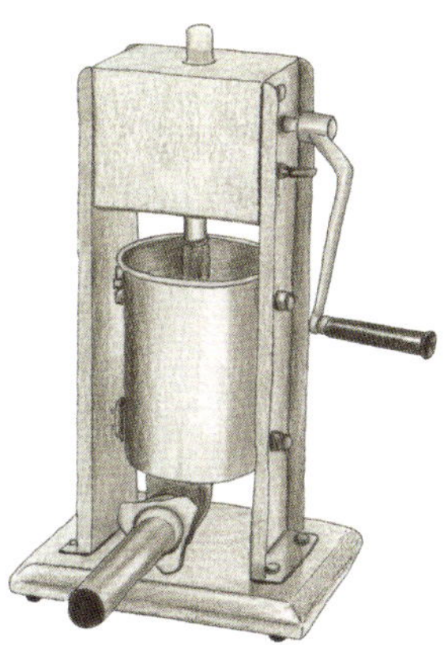

SAUSAGE STUFFER

This machine pushes meat into casings to become sausages.

PÂTÉ EN CROÛTE MOLD

This traditionally rectangular metal pan is equipped with a hinge that makes unmolding easier—but a standard loaf pan works as well.

CHARCUTERIE PREPARATIONS

◆ ◆ ◆

French charcuterie, with its vast array of seasoned meat-based preparations cooked in molds, terrines, saucepans, or casings, is arguably the most diverse in the world! Terrines, pâtés, pressed dishes, pâtés en croûte, rillettes, and sausages are a treat for gourmet connoisseurs.
In this book, we will focus on these preparations, rather than salted and smoked meats, blood sausages, and other recipes that are a bit too intricate to make at home.

THE DIFFERENT PREPARATIONS

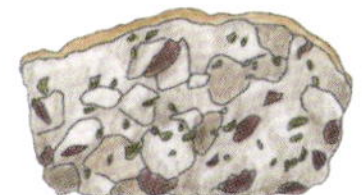

PÂTÉ

One or more finely ground meats are mixed, baked in a mold, and then cooled; this smooth-textured preparation is best enjoyed at room temperature.

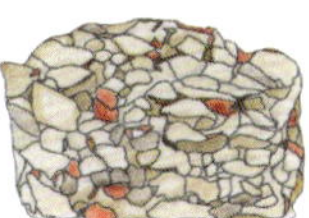

TERRINE

Closely related to pâté, a terrine primarily differs in how the ingredients are cut—usually in larger pieces.

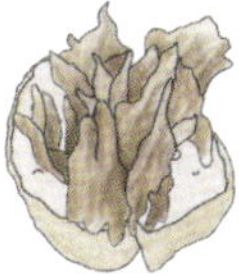

RILLETTES

Meat is cooked for a long time in its own fat, and then shredded. Rillettes can also be made with vegetables or fish.

PRESSED DISH

An assembly of ingredients cooked in a terrine, most often bound together by a flavored gelatin.

PÂTÉ EN CROÛTE

A pâté (or terrine) baked within a short-crust pastry or pie dough (see Workshop, p. 158), usually in a hinged metal mold. It can be served hot or at room temperature.

PIES & TORTES

Puff pastry wrapped around a seasoned filling, meant to be eaten hot.

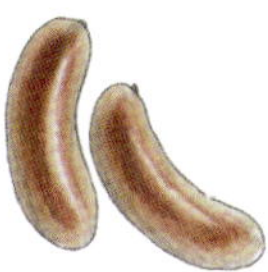

SAUSAGE

Ground meat enclosed in a casing, often enhanced with herbs, spices, or seasonings.

MEATS

◆ ◆ ◆

**Pork is undeniably the foundation of French charcuterie.
However, many other meats can be utilized as substitutions or accompaniments.
Each brings its unique touch.**

The ***SHOULDER*** is perfect for rillettes.

The ***BELLY***, with its tenderness, is ideal for pâtés and terrines.

The ***LEG*** is valued for its lean meat, especially in pâtés and terrines.

WHICH MEAT FOR WHAT PURPOSE?

DUCK

The breast is primarily used. Duck is often prepared similarly to chicken, and its bolder flavor enhances the character of charcuterie.

BEEF

Beef is not extensively used in charcuterie, but certain parts lend themselves well to charcuterie preparations. The melt-in-the-mouth cheek or the juicy flatiron steak can be turned into delightful rillettes or pressed dishes.

PHEASANT

Game birds and meat are commonly used in charcuterie; their distinctive gamey flavor broadens the aromatic spectrum, if kept in balance. For example, while wild boar can completely replace pork in pâtés and terrines, it's advisable to retain some pork for a rounded taste.

RABBIT

Rabbit is cherished for the mildness of its meat. Its use is similar to poultry; the legs are excellent for rillettes or pressed dishes, while the saddle complements a terrine.

VEAL

Veal, with its harmonious balance of lean and fat, is the best substitute for pork. For example, using veal breast in place of pork won't sacrifice the softness of stuffing, a pâté, or a terrine.

CHICKEN

Chicken is a favored accompaniment to pork. Its exceptionally lean meat makes it an easy ingredient to work with and combine. The breast, cut into cubes, is ideal for terrines and pâtés en croûte, while shredded legs are delicious in rillettes or pressed dishes.

CURING & SMOKING

◆ ◆ ◆

Cured and smoked meats are distinct charcuterie specialties, different from terrines, pâté en croûte, and rillettes due to their lack of casing and extended preservation.

WORKSHOP: CURING OR SMOKING?

Curing involves salting meat and allowing it to dry for varying durations. The salting can be applied via a dry rub or by brining (immersing the meat in a saltwater bath). Some examples of cured meat include Bayonne ham, Savoie ham, mountain sausage, and rosette sausage.

Smoking exposes food to smoke, altering its taste, texture, and color. Smoking can be done with raw meat, partially cooked meat, or previously salted meat. Some examples are smoked bacon, Black Forest ham, and Morteau sausage.

INCORPORATING CURED AND SMOKED MEAT INTO CHARCUTERIE

ADDING CHORIZO

Cubed chorizo (or sliced cured ham) can enhance a terrine; in fact, chorizo's robust and spicy nature harmonizes with many preparations.

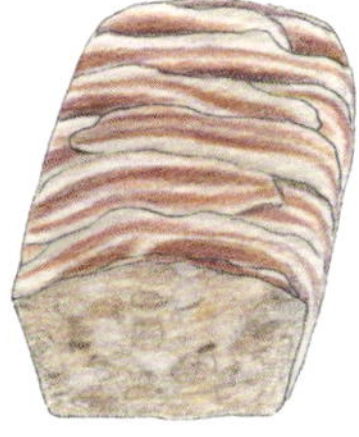

COVERING

Draping your pâté or terrine with thin slices of smoked bacon protects your dish during cooking and imparts a smoky flavor.

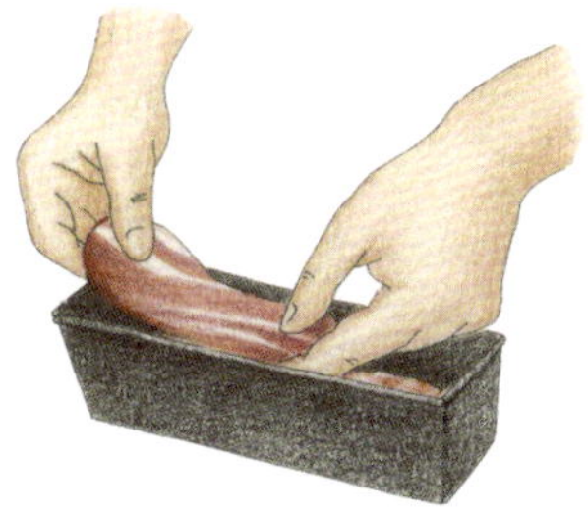

LAYERING

Dried pork tenderloin is a Corsican specialty. A layer added to a pressed dish can instill character.

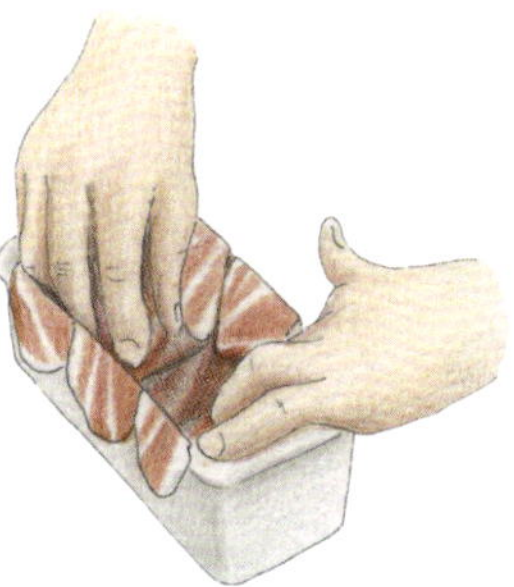

LINING WITH COPPA

Coppa, an iconic Italian charcuterie, can be used to line a pressed dish mold before assembly. The outcome is striking, both visually and gastronomically.

PÂTÉS

CHOPPING & MIXING

◆ ◆ ◆

Chopping and mixing meats are vital in the making of pâté. Chopping ensures a smooth and uniform result, while mixing guarantees the firmness required for the pâté, preventing it from crumbling. For example, mixing pork belly before integrating other ingredients leverages the natural collagen in the meat, achieving a well-formed slice.

WORKSHOP: CHOPPING, STEP BY STEP

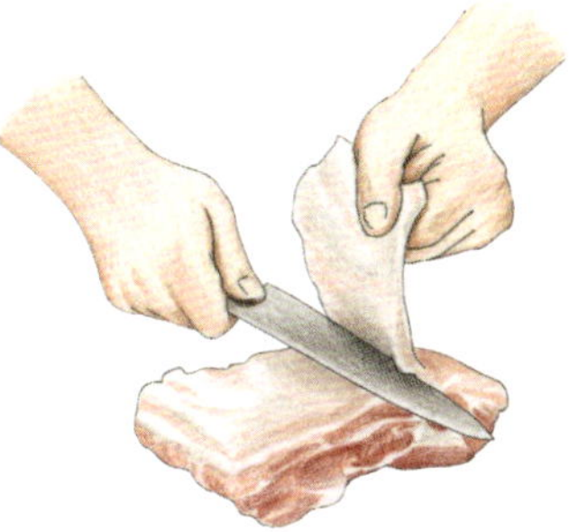

STEP 1

Remove the skin (or rind, for pork), leaving the fat.

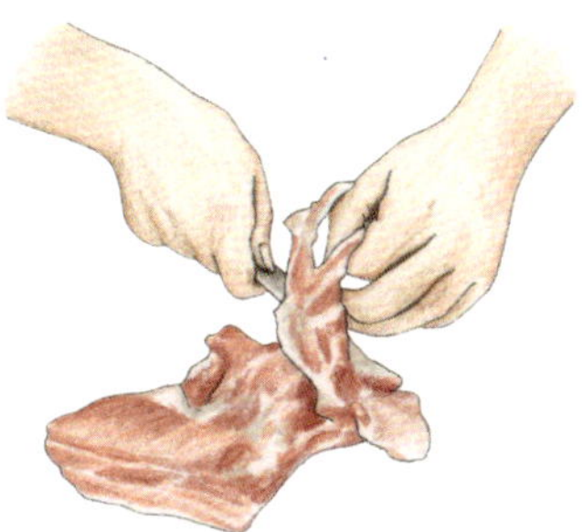

STEP 2

Remove bones if necessary.

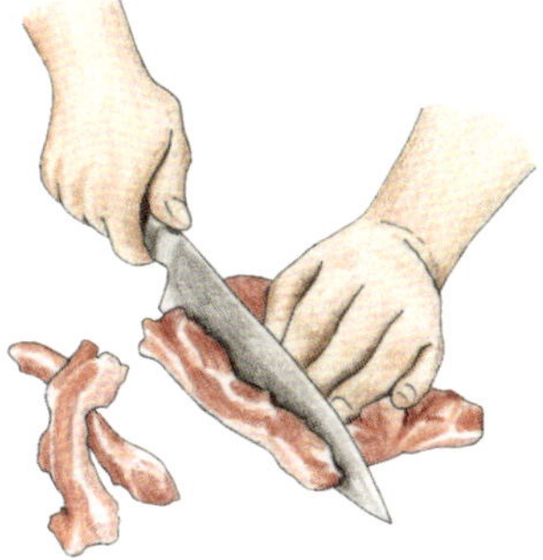

STEP 3

Using a chef's knife, slice the meat into thin lengths.

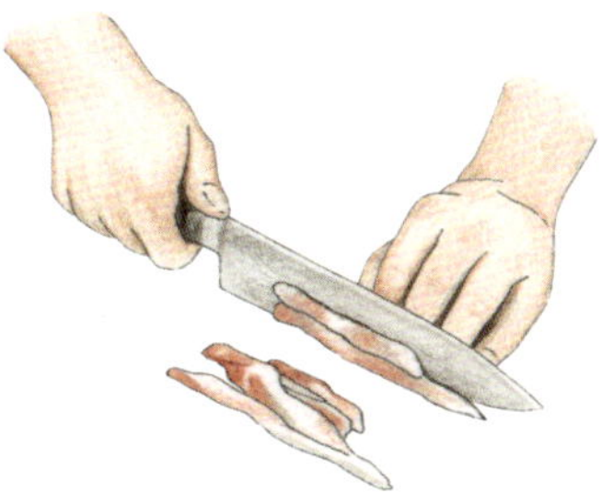

STEP 4

Cut the slices into strips.

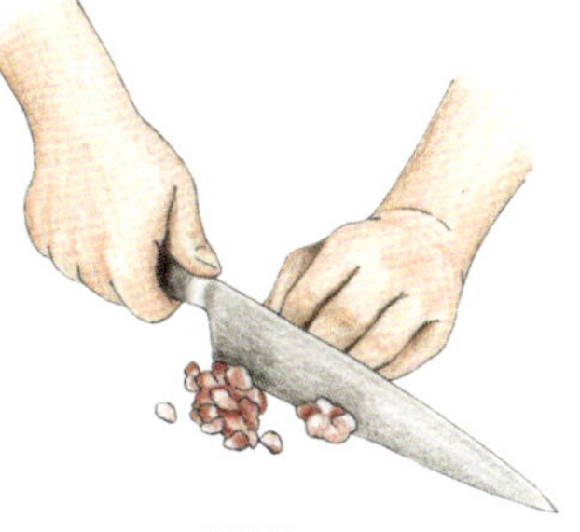

STEP 5

Dice the strips into small cubes, about ¼ inch (7 mm) on each side.

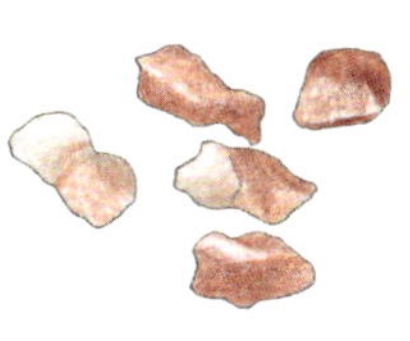

Pieces shown at actual size.

MIXING, STEP BY STEP

STEP 1

In a mixing bowl, flatten the chopped meat with your fist for 2 minutes.

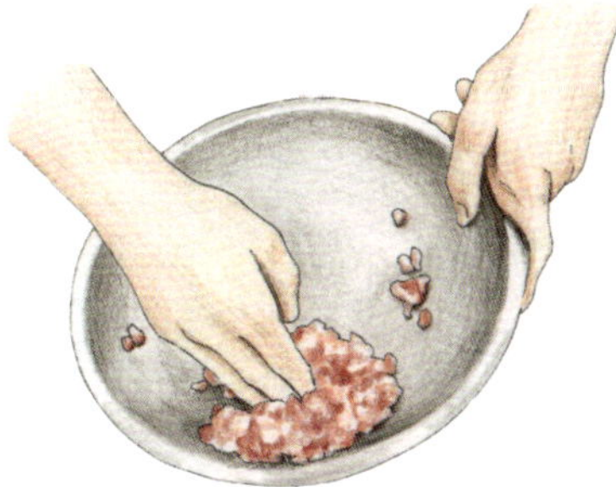

STEP 2

With your hands, mix thoroughly for about 5 minutes (or for 3 minutes on the lowest speed of a mixer) until the meat is sticky.

PREPARATION TIME
1 hour 30 minutes

COOKING TIME
1 hour 30 minutes

RESTING TIME
Overnight

COUNTRY PÂTÉ

◆ ◆ ◆

INGREDIENTS

1 ¼ pounds (650 g) whole pork belly or 1 pound (500 g) ground pork belly
½ pound (250 g) pork liver
½ large yellow onion
1 garlic clove
1 ½ shallots
6 sprigs parsley
1 tablespoon unsalted butter
3 teaspoons salt
4 pinches freshly ground pepper
2 large eggs, beaten
3 tablespoons plus 1 teaspoon heavy cream

MAKES 6 SERVINGS

Using a knife, remove the rind and any bones from the pork belly, making sure to keep the fat on the belly (see Workshop, p. 21). Chop the pork belly and pork liver into approximately ¼-inch (7 mm) pieces (see Workshop, p. 21); set aside.

Separately, chop the onion, garlic, shallot, and parsley leaves. In a skillet over medium heat, melt the butter and then add the onion. After a minute, add the garlic, shallot, and parsley, and sauté for about 3 minutes until everything becomes tender.

Place the ground pork belly in a mixing bowl. Add the salt and pepper and mix by hand (see Workshop, p. 21) or with a mixer on low speed. Pour the eggs and cream into the bowl and blend until the mixture becomes uniform.

Add the diced liver and sautéed vegetable mixture to the bowl. Vigorously mix by hand or in a mixer on low speed for 5 minutes. Transfer the mixture into a mold and press firmly.

Place the mold in a cold oven. Set the temperature to 320°F (160°C) and bake using the convection setting (if possible) for 1 hour 30 minutes.

Remove the mold, and while still hot, use a paper towel to dab away any imperfections on the pâté's edges. Let it rest for 1 hour at room temperature, then cover and refrigerate overnight. Remove from the refrigerator 30 minutes before serving.

Refrigerated leftovers will keep for 4 days.

STAUB
STAUB

PREPARATION TIME
1 hour 30 minutes

COOKING TIME
1 hour 30 minutes

RESTING TIME
Overnight

BRETON PÂTÉ

◆ ◆ ◆

INGREDIENTS

1 ½ pounds (750 g) whole pork belly or 1 pound (500 g) ground pork belly and ½ pound (200 g) pork rind
1 bottle (750 ml) red wine
2 bay leaves, divided
1 pound (500 g) pork liver
½ medium yellow onion
4 sprigs parsley
Leaves from 1 sprig thyme
3 teaspoons salt
5 pinches freshly ground pepper
2 large eggs
3 ½ tablespoons heavy cream

MAKES 6 SERVINGS

Using a knife, remove the rind and any bones from the pork belly, making sure to keep the fat on the belly (see Workshop, p. 21); reserve the rind. In a small saucepan, bring 2 ¼ cups (550 ml) of the red wine to a boil. Add 1 bay leaf and the pork rind, and gently simmer for 1 hour. It's adequately cooked when you can easily pierce the rind with a fork. Set aside.

Next, remove any membrane from the pork liver. Chop the pork belly and liver into approximately ¼-inch (7 mm) pieces (see Workshop, p. 21). Set aside.

Finely chop the onion, parsley leaves, thyme, and the remaining bay leaf and set aside. Place the chopped pork belly in a mixing bowl. Season with salt and pepper, then mix, either by hand or in a mixer on low speed (see Workshop, p. 21).

Pour the eggs and cream into the bowl and blend until the mixture becomes uniform. Add the pork liver, onion, parsley, bay leaf, thyme, and the remaining cup (200 ml) of red wine and mix for 2 more minutes.

Mince the cooked pork rind and then add it into the mixing bowl, combining vigorously either by hand or in a mixer on low speed for 5 minutes. Transfer the mixture to a mold and press firmly.

Place the mold in a cold oven. Set the oven to 320°F (160°C), and bake using the convection setting (if possible) for 1 hour 30 minutes.

Remove the mold, and while still hot, use a paper towel to dab away any imperfections on the pâté's edges. Let it rest for 1 hour at room temperature, then cover and refrigerate overnight. Remove from the refrigerator 30 minutes before serving.

Refrigerated leftovers will keep for 4 days.

PREPARATION TIME
1 hour 30 minutes

COOKING TIME
1 hour 30 minutes

RESTING TIME
Overnight

PÂTÉS

GRANDMA'S PÂTÉ

◆ ◆ ◆

INGREDIENTS

1 pound (500 g) pork belly
¾ pound (350 g) chicken livers
2 ounces (50 g) bread
6 sprigs parsley
2 shallots
½ cup (120 g) heavy cream
2 large eggs
3 teaspoons salt
4 pinches freshly ground pepper

MAKES 6 SERVINGS

Using a knife, remove the rind and any bones from the pork belly, making sure to keep the fat on the belly (see Workshop, p. 21).

Chop the pork belly and liver into approximately ¼-inch (7mm) pieces (see Workshop, p. 21).

Finely chop the parsley leaves and the shallots.

Pour the cream into a saucepan, add the bread, and cook over medium heat for 5 minutes. Add the parsley and shallots, and cook for an additional 2 minutes. Turn off heat and set aside.

Place the chopped pork belly in a mixing bowl. Add the salt and pepper. Mix by hand (see Workshop, p. 21) or with a mixer on low speed.

Add the eggs and mix until smooth. Add the chicken livers and the cream, bread, parsley, and shallot mixture. Stir vigorously by hand or with the mixer on low for 5 minutes, then transfer the mixture to a mold and press firmly.

Place the mold in a cold oven. Set the oven to 320°F (160°C) and bake using the convection setting (if possible) for 1 hour 30 minutes.

Remove the mold, and while still hot, use a paper towel to dab away any imperfections on the pâté's edges. Let it rest for 1 hour at room temperature, then cover and refrigerate overnight. Remove from the refrigerator 30 minutes before serving.

Refrigerate leftovers will keep for 4 days.

HANDMADE
IN SHEFFIELD

PREPARATION TIME
1 hour 30 minutes

COOKING TIME
1 hour 30 minutes

RESTING TIME
Overnight

PÂTÉS

RABBIT & HAZELNUT PÂTÉ

◆ ◆ ◆

INGREDIENTS

1 ¼ pounds (650 g) whole pork belly or 1 pound (500 g) chopped pork belly
2 ¼ pounds (1 kg) rabbit legs
⅓ pound (150 g) hazelnuts
3 teaspoons salt
4 pinches freshly ground pepper
1 large egg
¼ cup (60 g) heavy cream

MAKES 6 SERVINGS

Using a knife, remove the rind and any bones from the pork belly, making sure to keep the fat on the belly (see Workshop, p. 21). Chop the pork belly into approximately ¼-inch (7mm) pieces (see Workshop, p. 21).

Debone the rabbit legs and dice the pork belly into approximately ¼-inch (7 mm) pieces.

Halve the hazelnuts.

Place the chopped pork belly in a mixing bowl. Add the salt and pepper. Mix by hand (see Workshop, p. 21) or in a mixer on low speed.

Pour the egg and cream into the bowl and blend until the mixture becomes uniform. Add the rabbit and hazelnuts, and stir vigorously by hand or on a low speed for 5 minutes. Transfer the mixture to a mold and press firmly.

Place the mold in a cold oven. Set the temperature to 320°F (160°C) and bake using the convection setting (if possible) for 1 hour 30 minutes.

Remove the mold, and while still hot, use a paper towel to dab away any imperfections on the pâté's edges. Let it rest for 1 hour at room temperature, then cover and refrigerate overnight. Remove from the refrigerator 30 minutes before serving.

Refrigerated leftovers will keep for 4 days.

STAUB
STAUB

PREPARATION TIME
1 hour 30 minutes

COOKING TIME
1 hour 15 minutes

RESTING TIME
Overnight

PÂTÉS

DUCK & PEAR PÂTÉ

◆ ◆ ◆

INGREDIENTS

1 pear
1 ¼ pounds (650 g) whole pork belly or 1 pound (500 g) minced pork belly
1 ¾ pounds (800 g) skinless duck breast
3 teaspoons salt
5 pinches freshly ground pepper
1 large egg
¼ cup (60 g) heavy cream

MAKES 6 SERVINGS

Place the pear on a rimmed baking sheet, and place the sheet in a cold oven. Set the temperature to 320°F (160°C) and bake using the convection setting (if possible) for 30 minutes. Remove the pear, keeping the oven on.

While the pear cooks, using a knife, remove the rind and any bones from the pork belly, making sure to keep the fat on the belly (see Workshop, p. 21). Chop the pork belly and duck breast into ¼-inch (7mm) pieces (see Workshop, p. 21). Set aside.

Peel, core, and quarter the pear. Dice into ¼-inch (7 mm) cubes and set aside.

Place the pork belly in a mixing bowl, add the salt and pepper, and either mix by hand (see Workshop, p. 21) or with a mixer on low speed.

Pour the egg and cream into the bowl and blend until the mixture becomes uniform. Add the diced duck and pear to the mixture. Vigorously mix by hand or in a mixer on low speed for 5 minutes. Transfer the mixture into a mold and press firmly.

Place the mold in the oven and bake for 1 hour 15 minutes.

Remove the mold, and while still hot, use a paper towel to dab away any imperfections on the pâté's edges. Let it rest for 1 hour at room temperature, then cover and refrigerate overnight. Remove from the refrigerator 30 minutes before serving.

Refrigerated leftovers will keep for 4 days.

SPICES

ELEVATING CHARCUTERIE WITH

◆◆◆

Spices and charcuterie are the perfect pair. Moderation is crucial; in most recipes, the role of spices is to enhance the taste without overshadowing other ingredients. However, there are times when they take center stage, such as in the duck terrine with green peppercorns.

WHICH SPICE FOR WHAT PURPOSE?

PEPPER

The most commonly used spice in charcuterie is pepper (salt is not considered a spice). It gives character to dishes. Whether black, white, green, or even red, and regardless of its origin (like Penja, from Cameroon, or Kampot, from Cambodia), using freshly ground pepper is always recommended.

PAPRIKA

Often mild (though it can be hot or smoked), paprika can coat pâtés, terrines, pie crusts, and sausages. It lends a bell pepper-like taste, and helps even classic recipes burst with flavor.

NUTMEG

Nutmeg is a classic addition to pâtés and terrines, and gives a roundness to the flavor of the dish. Use it sparingly; you'll usually only need a pinch or two.

CINNAMON

Cinnamon is ideal for enhancing sweet-savory combinations, such as chicken and apple terrine.

CHILES

Often linked with Spanish charcuterie, chile peppers can also be used creatively in their French counterpart: terrines, rillettes, or sausages. From the milder Espelette to the spicier jalapeño or cayenne, the only limit is how much heat one can handle!

CURRY

A dash of curry powder can bring an exciting twist to a traditional dish. Chicken terrine with curry is always a hit!

PREPARATION TIME
1 hour 30 minutes

COOKING TIME
1 hour 30 minutes

RESTING TIME
Overnight

BASQUE PÂTÉ

◆ ◆ ◆

INGREDIENTS

1 ¼ pounds (650 g) whole pork belly or 1 pound (500 g) minced pork belly
1 ¼ pounds (650 g) boneless pork shoulder or 1 pound (500 g) minced pork shoulder
1 small fresh Espelette pepper or 1 teaspoon ground Espelette pepper.
3 teaspoons salt
3 pinches freshly ground pepper
1 large egg
¼ cup (60 g) heavy cream
¼ cup (50 g) cherry jam

MAKES 6 SERVINGS

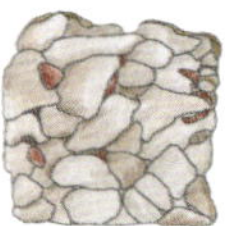

Using a knife, remove the rind and any bones from the pork belly, making sure to keep the fat on the belly (see Workshop, p. 21).

Chop the pork belly and pork shoulder into approximately ¼-inch (7mm) pieces (see Workshop, p. 21). Set aside.

If using fresh Espelette pepper, halve and remove the seeds, then chop finely. Make sure not to touch your eyes! Set aside.

Place the pork belly in a mixing bowl. Add the salt and pepper. Mix by hand (see Workshop, p. 21) or in a mixer on low speed.

Pour the egg and cream into the bowl and blend until the mixture becomes uniform. Add the minced pork shoulder, Espelette pepper, and cherry jam. Vigorously mix by hand or in a mixer on low speed for about 5 minutes. Transfer the mixture into a mold and press firmly.

Place the mold in a cold oven. Set the temperature to 320°F (160°F) and bake using the convection setting (if possible) for 1 hour 30 minutes.

Remove the mold, and while still hot, use a paper towel to dab away any imperfections on the pâté's edges. Let it rest for 1 hour at room temperature, then cover and refrigerate overnight. Remove from the refrigerator 30 minutes before serving.

Refrigerated leftovers will keep for 4 days.

PREPARATION TIME
1 hour 30 minutes

COOKING TIME
1 hour 30 minutes

RESTING TIME
Overnight

SUMMER PÂTÉ

◆ ◆ ◆

INGREDIENTS

1 pound (500 g) whole pork belly or 14 ounces (400 g) minced pork belly
1 pound (500 g) boneless skinless chicken breast
1 cup (200 g) black olives, divided
1 large egg
¼ cup (60 g) heavy cream
2 teaspoons herbes de Provence
3 teaspoons salt
4 pinches freshly ground pepper

MAKES 6 SERVING

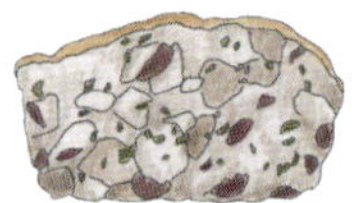

Using a knife, remove the rind and any bones from the pork belly, making sure to keep the fat on the belly (see Workshop, p. 21).

Chop the pork belly into approximately ¼-inch (7 mm) pieces (see Workshop, p. 21).

Dice the chicken and half the olives into approximately ¼-inch (7 mm) pieces.

In a blender, purée the remaining olives to a smooth consistency.

Place the pork belly in a mixing bowl; add the salt and pepper. Mix by hand (see Workshop, p. 21) or with a mixer on low speed.

Pour the egg and cream into the bowl and blend until the mixture becomes uniform. Add the chicken and the chopped and puréed olives and mix vigorously by hand (see Workshop, p. 21) or with a mixer on low speed for about 5 minutes. Transfer the mixture to a mold and press firmly.

Place the mold in a cold oven, set the temperature to 320°F (160°F) and bake using the convection setting (if possible) for 1 hour 30 minutes.

Remove the mold, and while still hot, use a paper towel to dab away any imperfections on the pâté's edges. Let it rest for 1 hour at room temperature, then cover and refrigerate overnight. Remove from the refrigerator 30 minutes before serving.

Refrigerated leftovers will keep for 4 days.

PREPARATION TIME
1 hour 30 minutes

COOKING TIME
1 hour 30 minutes

RESTING TIME
Overnight

PÂTÉS

CHICKEN PÂTÉ

◆ ◆ ◆

INGREDIENTS

1 ¼ pounds (650 g) whole pork belly or 1 pound (500 g) minced pork belly
6 sprigs parsley
1 ½ shallots
¼ cup (50 g) button mushrooms
1 tablespoon unsalted butter
3 teaspoons plus 1 pinch salt, divided
5 pinches freshly ground pepper
¼ pound (100 g) chicken livers
¾ pound (350 g) boneless skinless chicken breast
1 large egg
¼ cup plus 2 tablespoons (100 g) heavy cream

MAKES 6 SERVINGS

Using a knife, remove the rind and any bones from the pork belly, making sure to keep the fat on the belly (see Workshop, p. 21).

Finely chop parsley leaves. Dice the shallots and button mushrooms.

In a medium skillet over medium heat, melt the butter. Add shallots, mushrooms, and 1 pinch each of salt and pepper, stirring frequently. Once the shallots turn golden, add the parsley and chicken livers. Sauté until the livers have a rich brown color on both sides. Set aside to cool.

Chop the chicken and half the olives into approximately ¼-inch (7mm) pieces (see Workshop, p. 21).

Place the pork belly in a mixing bowl; add the remaining salt and pepper. Mix by hand (see Workshop, p. 21) or with a mixer on low speed.

Pour the egg and cream into the bowl and blend until the mixture becomes uniform. Add the livers, mushrooms, parsley, and shallots. Mix vigorously by hand or with a mixer on low speed for about 5 minutes. Transfer the mixture to a mold and press firmly.

Place the mold in a cold oven. Set the oven to 320°F (160°F) and bake using the convection setting (if possible) for 1 hour 30 minutes.

Remove the mold, and while still hot, use a paper towel to dab away any imperfections on the pâté's edges. Let it rest for 1 hour at room temperature, then cover and refrigerate overnight. Remove from the refrigerator 30 minutes before serving.

Refrigerated leftovers will keep for 4 days.

STAUB
STAUB

PREPARATION TIME
1 hour 30 minutes

COOKING TIME
1 hour 30 minutes

RESTING TIME
Overnight

PÂTÉS

FORÉZIEN PÂTÉ

◆ ◆ ◆

INGREDIENTS

1 pound (500 g) whole pork belly or 14 ounces (400 g) minced pork belly
¼ pound (150 g) chicken livers
½ yellow onion
8 sprigs parsley
1 pound (500 g) sausage meat
2 teaspoons salt
2 pinches freshly ground pepper
1 large egg
2 ¾ tablespoons heavy cream

MAKES 6 SERVINGS

Chop the pork belly and chicken livers into approximately ¼-inch (7mm) pieces (see Workshop, p. 21) and set aside.

Finely chop the onion and parsley leaves.

Place the sausage meat in a mixing bowl, add the salt and pepper, then mix by hand (see Workshop, p. 21) or in a mixer on low speed.

Pour the egg and cream into the bowl and blend until the mixture becomes uniform. Add the pork belly and chicken livers. Mix vigorously by hand or with a mixer on low speed for 5 minutes. Transfer the mixture to a mold, and press firmly.

Place the mold in a cold oven. Set the temperature to 320°F (160°F) and bake using the convection setting (if possible) for 1 hour 30 minutes.

Remove the mold, and while still hot, use a paper towel to dab away any imperfections on the pâté's edges. Let it rest for 1 hour at room temperature, then cover and refrigerate overnight. Remove from the refrigerator 30 minutes before serving.

Refrigerated leftovers will keep for 4 days.

PREPARATION TIME
1 hour

COOKING TIME
1 hour 30 minutes

RESTING TIME
Overnight

CAILLETTES

◆ ◆ ◆

INGREDIENTS

1 ¼ pounds (650 g) whole pork belly or 14 ounces (400 g) minced pork belly
½ pound (250 g) pork or veal liver
½ yellow onion
1 garlic clove
1 ½ shallots
½ bunch tarragon
20 sprigs parsley
1 tablespoon unsalted butter
3 ½ ounces (100 g) spinach
3 ½ tablespoons milk
3 teaspoons salt
4 pinches freshly ground pepper
1 large egg
3 ½ tablespoons heavy cream

MAKES 6 SERVINGS

Using a knife, remove the rind and any bones from the pork belly, making sure to keep the fat on the belly (see Workshop, p. 21).

Chop the pork belly and liver into approximately ¼-inch (7mm) pieces (see Workshop, p. 21). Set aside.

Finely chop the onion, garlic, shallot, tarragon, and parsley leaves. Set aside.

Roughly chop the spinach. In a medium skillet over medium heat, melt the butter, add the chopped spinach, and sauté for 3 minutes. Set aside.

In a small skillet, cook the onion and shallot with the milk over medium heat until soft.

Place the pork belly in a mixing bowl, add the salt and pepper, and mix by hand (see Workshop, p. 21) or with a mixer on low speed.

Pour the egg and cream into the bowl and blend until the mixture becomes uniform. Add the liver, milk-infused onion and shallot, and spinach, garlic, tarragon, and parsley to the bowl.

Mix vigorously by hand or with a mixer on low speed for 5 minutes. Divide the mixture into six portions, shape into balls, and place in six ramekins.

Put the ramekins in a cold oven. Set the oven to 320 °F (160 °C) and bake using the convection setting (if possible) for 1 hour 30 minutes.

Let the ramekins rest for 1 hour at room temperature, then cover and refrigerate overnight. Remove from the refrigerator 30 minutes before serving and unmold with the help of a knife.

Refrigerated leftovers will keep for 4 days.

PREPARATION TIME
1 hour 15 minutes

COOKING TIME
1 hour 30 minutes

RESTING TIME
Overnight

PÂTÉS

GUINEA FOWL PÂTÉ

◆ ◆ ◆

INGREDIENTS

1 ¼ pounds (650 g) whole pork belly or 14 ounces (400 g) minced pork belly
1 pound (500 g) guinea fowl breast
3 teaspoons salt
4 pinches freshly ground pepper
1 large egg
¼ cup (60 g) heavy cream

MAKES 6 SERVINGS

Using a knife, remove the rind and any bones from the pork belly, making sure to keep the fat on the belly (see Workshop, p. 21).

Chop the pork belly into approximately ¼-inch (7mm) pieces (see Workshop, p. 21).

Dice the pork belly into approximately ¼-inch (7 mm) pieces.

Place the pork belly in a mixing bowl. Add the salt and pepper, then mix by hand or in a mixer on low speed.

Pour the egg and cream into the bowl and blend until the mixture becomes uniform. Add the guinea fowl, mixing vigorously by hand or in a mixer on low speed for 5 minutes. Transfer the mixture into a mold and press firmly.

Place the mold in a cold oven. Set the oven to 320°F (160°F) and bake using the convection setting (if possible) for 1 hour 30 minutes.

Remove the mold, and while still hot, use a paper towel to dab away any imperfections on the pâté's edges. Let it rest for 1 hour at room temperature, then cover and refrigerate overnight. Remove from the refrigerator 30 minutes before serving.

Refrigerated leftovers will keep for 4 days.

PREPARATION TIME
15 minutes

RESTING TIME
24 hours

PÂTÉS

PICKLES

◆ ◆ ◆

INGREDIENTS

¼ small cauliflower
4 spring onions
4 carrots
1 bunch small radishes
1 cup (200 g) granulated sugar
1 ¾ cups (400 g) sherry or red wine vinegar
3 ½ cups (800 g) water

Clean and scrub the vegetables. Divide the cauliflower into florets. Remove the stems from the spring onions and quarter them. Slice the carrots into sticks (or rings) and trim the radishes, keeping them whole.

Arrange the vegetables in clean or sterilized jars, choosing jars based on the total volume of the vegetables to fill them entirely.

In a saucepan, combine sugar and vinegar, and bring to a boil. Pour the hot liquid over the vegetables, ensuring they are completely submerged.

Seal the jars tightly and allow them to cool at room temperature.

Refrigerate for 24 hours before serving with pâtés, terrines, or rillettes. Refrigerated pickles will keep for 1 to 2 months.

TERRINES

CUBING MEAT

◆ ◆ ◆

Cutting meat into rough cubes accentuates its taste and enhances its texture when eaten in a terrine. This blend of larger pieces of meat is the primary distinction between terrines and pâtés.
In pâtés, meats are finely minced.

WORKSHOP: CUBING

STEP 1

Equip yourself with a well-sharpened chef's knife.

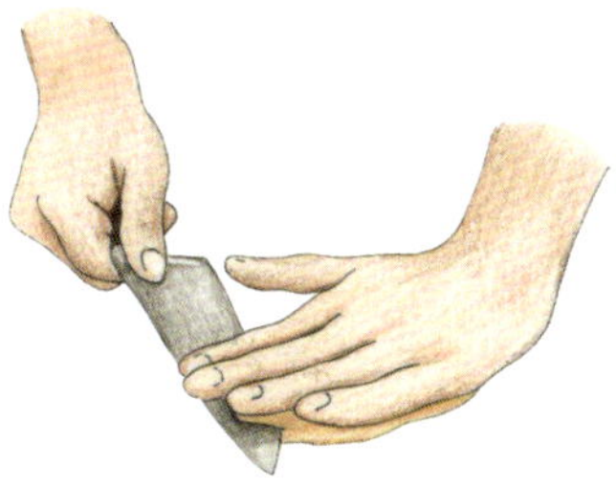

STEP 2

With the knife, slice the chicken breast in half horizontally.

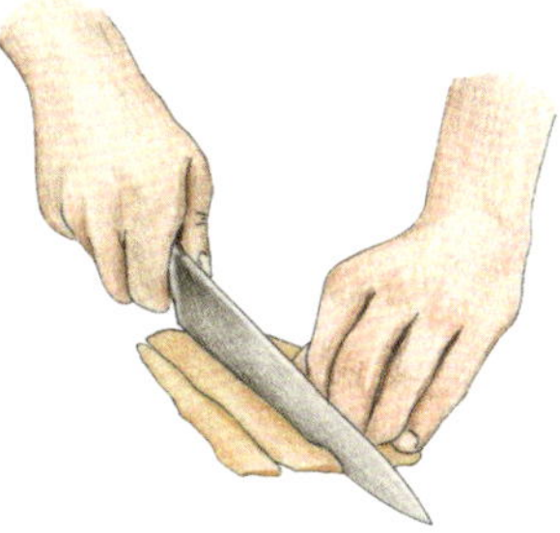

STEP 3

Slice each half lengthwise into strips.

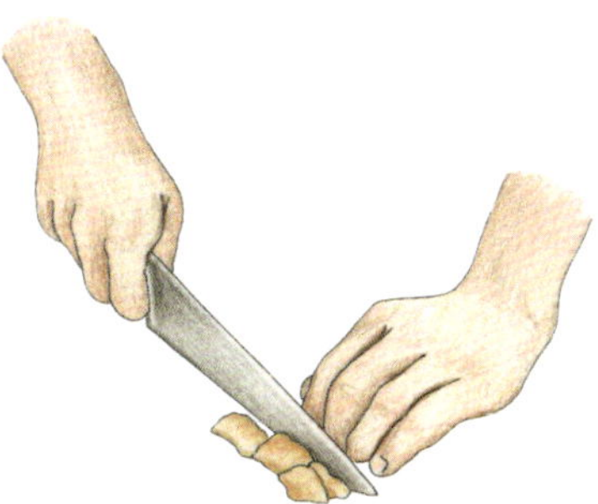

STEP 4

Cut the resulting strips crosswise into cubes.

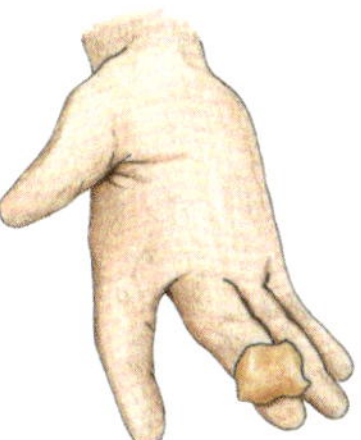

STEP 5

The ideal cube size is roughly ½ inch (1 ¼ cm) per side.

Pieces shown at actual size.

PREPARATION TIME
50 minutes

COOKING TIME
1 hour 30 minutes

RESTING TIME
Overnight

RABBIT WITH MUSTARD TERRINE

◆◆◆

INGREDIENTS

1 ¼ pounds (650 g) whole pork belly or 14 ounces (400 g) minced pork belly
2 ¼ pounds (1 kg) rabbit legs
3 teaspoons salt
4 pinches freshly ground pepper
1 large egg
¼ cup (60 g) heavy cream
3 tablespoons brown or Dijon mustard

MAKES 6 SERVINGS

Using a knife, remove the rind and any bones from the pork belly, making sure to keep the fat on the belly (see Workshop, p. 21). Chop the pork belly into approximately ¼-inch (7mm) pieces (see Workshop, p. 21).

Debone the rabbit legs and cut into ½-inch (1 ½ cm) cubes (see Workshop, p. 51).

Place the pork belly in a mixing bowl, add the salt and pepper, then mix by hand or with a mixer on low speed.

Pour the egg and cream into the bowl and blend until the mixture becomes uniform. Add the rabbit and mustard, stirring vigorously either by hand (see Workshop, p. 21) or with a mixer on low speed for 5 minutes.

Transfer the mixture to a mold and press firmly.

Place the mold in a cold oven. Set the oven to 320°F (160°C) and bake using the convection setting (if possible) for 1 hour 30 minutes.

Remove the mold, and while still hot, use a paper towel to dab away any imperfections on the terrine's edges. Let it rest for 1 hour at room temperature, then cover and refrigerate overnight. Remove from the refrigerator 30 minutes before serving.

Refrigerated leftovers will keep for 4 days.

PREPARATION TIME
1 hour 30 minutes

COOKING TIME
1 hour 30 minutes

RESTING TIME
Overnight

APPLE & CIDER TERRINE

◆ ◆ ◆

INGREDIENTS

1 pound (500 g) whole pork belly or 14 ounces (400 g) minced pork belly
1 pound (500 g) boneless skinless chicken breast
1 apple
1 tablespoon unsalted butter
1 tablespoon granulated sugar
⅔ cup (150 grams) apple cider
3 teaspoons salt
4 pinches freshly ground pepper
1 large egg
¼ cup (60 g) heavy cream

MAKES 6 SERVINGS

Using a knife, remove the rind and any bones from the pork belly, making sure to keep the fat on the belly (see Workshop, p. 21). Chop the pork belly into approximately ¼-inch (7mm) pieces (see Workshop, p. 21).

Cut the chicken breast into approximately ½-inch (1 ½ cm cm) cubes (see Workshop, p. 51).

Peel, core, and quarter the apple. Chop into approximately ¼-inch (7 mm) pieces.

In a large skillet over medium heat, melt the butter. Add the apple pieces and stir for 2 minutes. Sprinkle in the sugar and continue stirring until the apples are slightly caramelized. Add the cider and chicken and continue stirring for another 30 seconds.

In a mixing bowl, combine the chopped pork belly with salt and pepper. Mix by hand (see Workshop, p. 21) or in a mixer on low speed.

Pour the egg and cream into the bowl and blend until the mixture becomes uniform. Add the apple-chicken mixture to the bowl and mix thoroughly either by hand or in a mixer on low speed for 5 minutes.

Transfer the mixture into a mold and press firmly. Place the mold in a cold oven. Set the temperature to 320°F (160°F) and bake using the convection setting (if possible) for 1 hour 30 minutes.

Remove the mold, and while still hot, use a paper towel to dab away any imperfections on the terrine's edges. Let it rest for 1 hour at room temperature, then cover and refrigerate overnight. Remove from the refrigerator 30 minutes before serving.

Refrigerated leftovers will keep for 4 days.

PREPARATION TIME
1 hour 30 minutes

COOKING TIME
15 minutes + 1 hour 30 minutes

RESTING TIME
Overnight

CHICKEN, BELL PEPPER, TOMATO TERRINE

◆ ◆ ◆

INGREDIENTS

1 pound (500 g) whole pork belly or 14 ounces (400 g) minced pork belly
2 small (250 g) red bell peppers
1 medium (200 g) vine tomato
Olive oil, for drizzling
3 teaspoons plus 1 pinch salt
5 pinches freshly ground pepper
14 ounces (400 g) boneless skinless chicken breast
1 large egg
¼ cup (60 g) heavy cream

MAKES 6 SERVINGS

Preheat the oven to 300°F (150°C). Using a knife, remove the rind and any bones from the pork belly, making sure to keep the fat on the belly (see Workshop, p. 21). Chop the pork belly into approximately ¼-inch (7mm) pieces (see Workshop, p. 21). Quarter the bell peppers, removing seeds and white membranes. Quarter the tomato, discarding the stem and seeds, keeping only the flesh.

Transfer the peppers and tomato to a baking sheet; drizzle with olive oil and season with 1 pinch each of the salt and pepper. Place sheet in the oven and bake for 15 minutes. Let vegetables cool to room temperature, and then peel off and discard their skins. Chop the vegetables into ⅕-inch (5 mm) pieces.

Cut the chicken breast into approximately ½-inch (1 ½) cubes (see Workshop, p. 51).

In a mixing bowl, combine the minced pork belly and the remaining 3 teaspoons salt and 4 pinches pepper. Mix either by hand (see Workshop, p. 21) or in a mixer at a low speed.

Pour the egg and cream into the bowl and blend until the mixture becomes uniform. Fold in the chicken, tomato, and bell peppers. Mix thoroughly either by hand or in a mixer on low speed for 5 minutes. Transfer the mixture into a mold and press firmly.

Place the mold in a cold oven, set the temperature to 320°F (160°F), and bake using the convection setting (if possible) for 1 hour 30 minutes.

Remove the mold, and while still hot, use a paper towel to dab away any imperfections on the terrine's edges. Let it rest for 1 hour at room temperature, then refrigerate overnight. Remove from the refrigerator 30 minutes before serving.

Refrigerated leftovers will keep for 4 days.

PREPARATION TIME
50 minutes

COOKING TIME
1 hour 30 minutes

RESTING TIME
Overnight

DUCK WITH GREEN PEPPERCORNS TERRINE

◆ ◆ ◆

INGREDIENTS

1 ¼ pounds (650 g) whole pork belly or 14 ounces (400 g) minced pork belly
1 ¾ pounds (800 g) duck breast
3 teaspoons salt
2 pinches freshly ground pepper
1 large egg
¼ cup (60 g) heavy cream
2 teaspoons whole green peppercorns

MAKES 6 SERVINGS

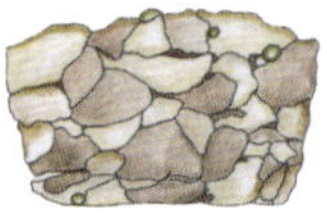

Using a knife, remove the rind and any bones from the pork belly, making sure to keep the fat on the belly (see Workshop, p. 21). Chop the pork belly into approximately ¼-inch (7mm) pieces (see Workshop, p. 21). Remove the skin from the duck breast and cut the breast into cubes of roughly ⅗ inch (1 ¾ cm).

Place the pork belly in a mixing bowl. Add the salt and pepper, then mix by hand (see Workshop, p. 21) or in a mixer on low speed.

Pour the egg and cream into the bowl and blend until the mixture is uniform. Add the duck breast cubes and whole green peppercorns.

Mix vigorously by hand or in a mixer on low speed for 5 minutes. Transfer the mixture into a mold and press firmly.

Place the mold in a cold oven, set the temperature to 320°F (160 °C), and bake using the convection setting (if possible) for 1 hour 30 minutes.

Remove the mold, and while still hot, use a paper towel to dab away any imperfections on the terrine's edges. Let it rest for 1 hour at room temperature, then cover and refrigerate overnight. Remove from the refrigerator 30 minutes before serving.

Refrigerated leftovers will keep for 4 days.

PREPARATION TIME
1 hour

COOKING TIME
1 hour 30 minutes

RESTING TIME
Overnight

TERRINES

DUCK & APRICOTS TERRINE

◆ ◆ ◆

INGREDIENTS

1 ¼ pounds (650 g) whole pork belly or 14 ounces (400 g) minced pork belly
1 ¾ pounds (800 g) duck breast
4 ½ ounces (125 g) dried apricots
3 teaspoons salt
4 pinches freshly ground pepper
3 large eggs
¼ cup (60 g) heavy cream

MAKES 6 SERVINGS

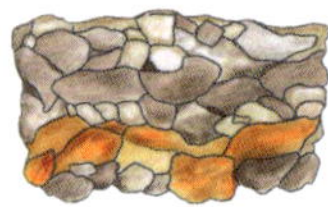

Using a knife, remove the rind and any bones from the pork belly, making sure to keep the fat on the belly (see Workshop, p. 21). Chop the pork belly into approximately ¼-inch (7mm) pieces (see Workshop, p. 21).

Remove the skin from the duck breast and cut the breast into cubes of roughly ⅗ inch (1 ¾ cm).

Cut the dried apricots into cubes of roughly ⅗ inch (1 ¾ cm).

Place the pork belly in a mixing bowl. Add the salt and pepper, then mix by hand (see Workshop, p. 21) or with a mixer on low speed.

Pour the eggs and cream into the bowl, and mix until uniform. Add the apricots and duck. Vigorously mix by hand or in a mixer on low speed for 5 minutes. Transfer the mixture into a mold and press down firmly.

Place the mold in a cold oven. Set the temperature to 320°F (160 °C) and bake using the convection setting (if possible) for 1 hour 30 minutes.

Remove the mold, and while still hot, use a paper towel to dab away any imperfections on the terrine's edges. Let it rest for 1 hour at room temperature, then cover and refrigerate overnight. Remove from the refrigerator 30 minutes before serving.

Refrigerated leftovers will keep for 4 days.

MADE IN SPAIN

PREPARATION TIME
1 hour

COOKING TIME
1 hour 30 minutes

RESTING TIME
Overnight

TERRINES

ALL PORK

◆ ◆ ◆

INGREDIENTS

1 pound (500 g) whole pork belly or 14 ounces (400 g) minced pork belly
1 pound (500 g) boneless pork shoulder
5 ¼ ounces (150 g) chopped bacon
3 teaspoons salt
1 teaspoon whole peppercorns
1 pinch freshly ground pepper
1 large egg
¼ cup (60 g) heavy cream

MAKES 6 SERVINGS

Using a knife, remove the rind and any bones from the pork belly, making sure to keep the fat on the belly (see Workshop, p. 21). Chop the pork belly into approximately ¼-inch (7mm) pieces (see Workshop, p. 21).

Cut the pork shoulder into approximately ⅗-inch (1 ¾-cm) cubes.

In a medium pan over medium heat, cook the bacon for 1 minute, until lightly browned.

Place the pork belly in a mixing bowl. Add the salt and both types of pepper, and mix by hand (see Workshop, p. 21) or with a mixer on low speed.

Pour the egg and cream into the bowl, and blend until the mixture becomes uniform. Add the pork shoulder and bacon. Vigorously mix by hand or in a mixer on low speed for 5 minutes. Transfer the mixture to a mold and press firmly.

Place the mold in a cold oven. Set the thermostat to 320°F (160 °C) and bake using the convection setting (if possible) for 1 hour 30 minutes.

Remove the mold, and while still hot, use a paper towel to dab away any imperfections on the terrine's edges. Let it rest for 1 hour at room temperature, then cover and refrigerate overnight. Remove from the refrigerator 30 minutes before serving.

Refrigerated leftovers will keep for 4 days.

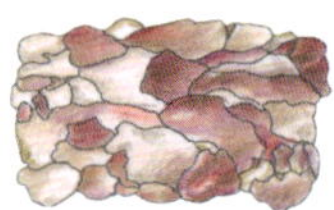

PREPARATION TIME	COOKING TIME	RESTING TIME
1 hour 10 minutes	1 hour 30 minutes	Overnight

QUÉBÉCOIS TERRINE

◆ ◆ ◆

INGREDIENTS

½ cup (100 g) dried cranberries
1 ⅓ cups (330 g) pale ale or blond beer
1 ¼ pounds (650 g) whole pork belly or 14 ounces (400 g) minced pork belly
14 ounces (400 g) boneless pork shoulder or 14 ounces (400 g) minced pork shoulder
3 teaspoons salt
4 pinches freshly ground pepper
1 large egg
¼ cup (60 g) heavy cream

MAKES 6 SERVINGS

Place the cranberries in a large glass and pour the beer over them.

Using a knife, remove the rind and any bones from the pork belly, making sure to keep the fat on the belly (see Workshop, p. 21). Chop the pork belly into approximately ¼-inch (7mm) pieces (see Workshop, p. 21).

Cut the pork shoulder into approximately ½-inch (1 ½-cm) cubes (see Workshop, p. 51).

Place the pork belly in a mixing bowl, add the salt and pepper, and mix by hand (see Workshop, p. 21) or with a mixer on low speed.

Pour the egg and cream into the bowl and blend until the mixture becomes uniform.

Add the soaked cranberries, half the beer, and the pork shoulder to the bowl. Mix vigorously by hand or in a mixer on low speed for about 5 minutes. Transfer the mixture to a mold and press firmly.

Place the mold in a cold oven. Set the temperature to 320°F (160°C) and cook using the convection setting (if possible) for 1 hour 30 minutes.

Remove the mold, and while still hot, use a paper towel to dab away any imperfections on the terrine's edges. Let it rest for 1 hour at room temperature, then cover and refrigerate overnight. Remove from the refrigerator 30 minutes before serving.

Refrigerated leftovers will keep for 4 days.

PREPARATION TIME
1 hour 10 minutes

COOKING TIME
1 hour 30 minutes

RESTING TIME
Overnight

TERRINE FOR ALL

◆ ◆ ◆

INGREDIENTS

1 ½ pounds (750 g) whole veal breast or 1 pound (500 g) minced veal breast
⅔ pound (300 g) boneless skinless chicken breast
14 ounces (400 g) duck confit
3 teaspoons salt
4 pinches freshly ground pepper
1 large egg
¼ cup (60 g) heavy cream

MAKES 6 SERVINGS

Using a knife, remove the skin and any bones from the veal breast, making sure to keep the fat. Chop the veal into approximately ¼-inch (7mm) pieces (see Workshop, p. 21).

Cut the chicken breast into roughly ½-inch (1 ½-cm) cubes (see Workshop, p. 51).

Remove the skin and bones from the duck confit and shred it by hand (see Workshop, p. 109).

Place the veal breast in a mixing bowl, add the salt and pepper, and mix by hand or on with a mixer on low speed.

Pour the egg and cream into the bowl and mix until uniform. Add the chicken and duck, mixing vigorously by hand or with a mixer on low speed for about 5 minutes. Transfer the mixture to a mold and press firmly.

Place the mold in a cold oven. Set the temperature to 320°F (160°C) and cook using the convection setting (if possible) for 1 hour 30 minutes.

Remove the mold, and while still hot, use a paper towel to dab away any imperfections on the terrine's edges. Let it rest for 1 hour at room temperature, then cover and refrigerate overnight. Remove from the refrigerator 30 minutes before serving.

Refrigerated leftovers will keep for 4 days.

PREPARATION TIME
1 hour

COOKING TIME
1 hour 30 minutes

RESTING TIME
Overnight

TERRINES

ELEGANT FOWL TERRINE

◆ ◆ ◆

INGREDIENTS

1 ¼ pounds (650 g) whole pork belly or 14 ounces (400 g) minced pork belly
1 pound (500 g) duck breast
½ pound (250 g) boneless skinless chicken breast
3 teaspoons salt
4 pinches freshly ground pepper
1 large egg
¼ cup (60 g) heavy cream

MAKES 6 SERVINGS

Using a knife, remove the rind and any bones from the pork belly, making sure to keep the fat on the belly (see Workshop, p. 21). Chop the pork belly into approximately ¼-inch (7mm) pieces (see Workshop, p. 21).

Remove the skin from the duck breast. Cut the duck and the chicken breast into roughly ½-inch (1 ½-cm) cubes (see Workshop, p. 51).

Transfer the pork belly into a large mixing bowl, add the salt and pepper, and mix by hand (see Workshop, p. 21) or with a mixer on low speed.

Pour the egg and cream into the bowl and mix until uniform. Add the duck and chicken and continue mixing by hand or with a mixer on low speed for about 5 minutes. Transfer the mixture to a mold and press firmly.

Place the mold in a cold oven. Set the temperature to 320°F (160°C) and bake using the convection setting (if possible) for 1 hour 30 minutes.

Remove the mold, and while still hot, use a paper towel to dab away any imperfections on the terrine's edges. Let it rest for 1 hour at room temperature, then cover and refrigerate overnight. Remove from the refrigerator 30 minutes before serving.

Refrigerated leftovers will keep for 4 days.

PREPARATION TIME
1 hour 15 minutes

COOKING TIME
1 hour 30 minutes

RESTING TIME
Overnight

TERRINES

CARAMELIZED PORK TERRINE

◆ ◆ ◆

INGREDIENTS

1 ¼ pounds (650 g) whole pork belly or 14 ounces (400 g) minced pork belly
14 ounces (400 g) boneless pork shoulder
2 teaspoons salt
4 pinches freshly ground pepper
1 large egg
¼ cup (60 g) heavy cream
3 tablespoons water
3 tablespoons granulated sugar
1 tablespoon soy sauce

MAKES 6 SERVINGS

Using a knife, remove the rind and any bones from the pork belly, making sure to keep the fat on the belly (see Workshop, p. 21). Cube the pork belly into approximately ½-inch (1 ½ cm) pieces (see Workshop, p. 51).

Cut the pork shoulder into roughly ½-inch (1 ½-cm) cubes (see Workshop, p. 51).

Transfer the minced pork belly to a large mixing bowl, season with the salt and pepper, and either mix by hand (see Workshop, p. 21) or with a mixer on low speed.

Pour the egg and cream into the bowl and mix until uniform.

In a large skillet, heat the water over high heat. Once it's hot, add the sugar, stirring with a wooden spoon until it begins to caramelize. Reduce the heat to medium, add the soy sauce and pork shoulder, and stir for another minute.

Pour the skillet's contents into the mixing bowl with the pork belly. Mix the ingredients either by hand (see Workshop, p. 21) or with a mixer on low speed for about 5 minutes. Transfer the mixture to a mold and press firmly.

Place the mold in a cold oven. Set the temperature to 320°F (160°C) and bake using the convection setting (if possible) for 1 hour 30 minutes.

Remove the mold, and while still hot, use a paper towel to dab away any imperfections on the terrine's edges. Let it rest for 1 hour at room temperature, then cover and refrigerate overnight. Remove from the refrigerator 30 minutes before serving.

Refrigerated leftovers will keep for 4 days.

PREPARATION TIME
1 hour

COOKING TIME
1 hour 30 minutes

RESTING TIME
Overnight

BLUE CHEESE TERRINE

◆ ◆ ◆

INGREDIENTS

1 pound (500 g) whole pork belly or 14 ounces (400 g) minced pork belly
14 ounces (400 g) boneless pork shoulder or 14 ounces (400 g) minced pork shoulder
⅔ cup (150 g) blue cheese
3 teaspoons salt
4 pinches freshly ground pepper
1 large egg
¼ cup (60 g) heavy cream

MAKES 6 SERVINGS

Using a knife, remove the rind and any bones from the pork belly, making sure to keep the fat on the belly (see Workshop, p. 21). Cube the pork belly into approximately ½-inch (1 ½ cm) pieces (see Workshop, p. 51).

Cut the pork shoulder into roughly ½-inch (1 ½-cm) cubes and the blue cheese into ¼-inch (7- mm) dice.

Place the pork belly in a mixing bowl. Add the salt and pepper and mix by hand (see Workshop, p. 21) or in a mixer on low speed.

Pour the egg and cream into the bowl and mix until uniform.

Add the pork shoulder and cheese to the mixture. Vigorously mix by hand or in a mixer at low speed for about 5 minutes. Transfer the mixture to a mold and press firmly.

Place the mold in a cold oven. Set the temperature to 320°F (160°C) and bake using the convection setting (if possible) for 1 hour 30 minutes.

Remove the mold, and while still hot, use a paper towel to dab away any imperfections on the terrine's edges. Let it rest for 1 hour at room temperature, then cover and refrigerate overnight. Remove from the refrigerator 30 minutes before serving.

Refrigerated leftovers will keep for 4 days.

PREPARATION TIME
1 hour 30 minutes

COOKING TIME
1 hour 30 minutes

RESTING TIME
Overnight

TERRINES

THREE MEATS & PISTACHIOS TERRINE

◆ ◆ ◆

INGREDIENTS

1 pound (500 g) whole pork belly or 14 ounces (400 g) minced pork belly
⅓ pound (150 g) boneless pork shoulder
⅓ pound (150 g) veal nut (or veal round)
⅓ pound (150 g) boneless skinless chicken breast
3 teaspoons salt
4 pinches freshly ground pepper
1 large egg
¼ cup (60 g) heavy cream
½ cup (70 g) shelled pistachios

MAKES 6 SERVINGS

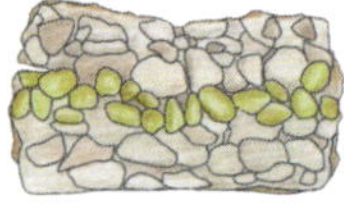

Using a knife, remove the rind and any bones from the pork belly, making sure to keep the fat on the belly (see Workshop, p. 21). Chop the pork belly into approximately ¼-inch (7mm) pieces (see Workshop, p. 21).

Cut the pork shoulder, veal nut, and chicken breast into roughly ½-inch (1 ½-cm) cube (see Workshop, p. 51).

Place the pork belly in a mixing bowl, add the salt and pepper, and mix by hand (see Workshop p. 21) or with a mixer on low speed.

Pour the egg and cream into the bowl and mix until uniform.

Add the pork shoulder, veal, and chicken. Mix by hand or with the mixer on low for 5 minutes.

Pour half of the mixture into a mold, press firmly, top with a layer of the pistachios, and then add the remaining mixture. Press down once more.

Place the mold in a cold oven. Set the temperature to 320°F (160 °C) and bake using the convection setting (if possible) for 1 hour 30 minutes.

Remove the mold, and while still hot, use a paper towel to dab away any imperfections on the terrine's edges. Let it rest for 1 hour at room temperature, then cover and refrigerate overnight. Remove from the refrigerator 30 minutes before serving.

Refrigerated leftovers will keep for 4 days.

PREPARATION TIME
1 hour 30 minutes

COOKING TIME
1 hour 30 minutes

RESTING TIME
Overnight

FOREST TERRINE

◆ ◆ ◆

INGREDIENTS

1 pound (500 g) whole pork belly or 14 ounces (400 g) minced pork belly
14 ounces (400 g) boneless skinless chicken breast
6 sprigs parsley
1 shallot
½ cup (50 g) oyster mushrooms
½ cup (50 g) white button mushrooms
1 tablespoon unsalted butter
3 teaspoons plus 1 pinch salt
5 pinches freshly ground pepper
1 large egg
¼ cup (60 g) heavy cream

MAKES 6 SERVINGS

Using a knife, remove the rind and any bones from the pork belly, making sure to keep the fat on the belly (see Workshop, p. 21). Chop the pork belly into approximately ¼-inch (7mm) pieces (see Workshop, p. 21).

Cut the chicken breast into roughly ½-inch (1 ½ cm) cubes (see Workshop, p. 51).

Finely chop the parsley leaves and shallot. Clean the mushrooms and quarter them.

In a medium skillet over medium heat, melt the butter, then add the shallot, mushrooms, and 1 pinch each of the salt and pepper. Stir until the mushrooms are lightly browned. Add the parsley, stirring for about 30 seconds, and then remove from the heat. Once slightly cooled, dice the mushrooms into approximately ¼-inch (7 mm) pieces and set aside.

In a mixing bowl, combine the minced pork belly with the remaining 3 teaspoons salt and 4 pinches pepper, either by hand (see Workshop, p. 21) or in a mixer on low speed.

Pour the egg and cream into the bowl and mix until uniform. Add the mushrooms, shallot, parsley, and chicken, mixing vigorously for 5 minutes.

Transfer the mixture to a mold and press firmly.

Place the mold in a cold oven. Set the temperature to 320°F (160 °C) and bake using the convection setting (if possible) for 1 hour 30 minutes.

Remove the mold, and while still hot, use a paper towel to dab away any imperfections on the terrine's edges. Let it rest for 1 hour at room temperature, then cover and refrigerate overnight. Remove from the refrigerator 30 minutes before serving.

Refrigerated leftovers will keep for 4 days.

PREPARATION TIME
1 hour 15 minutes

COOKING TIME
1 hour 30 minutes

RESTING TIME
Overnight

TERRINES

DUCK WITH PISTACHIOS TERRINE

◆ ◆ ◆

INGREDIENTS

1 ¼ pounds (650 g) whole pork belly or 1 pound (500 g) minced pork belly
1 ¾ pounds (800 g) duck breast
⅓ cup (150 g) shelled pistachios
4 teaspoons fine salt
4 pinches freshly ground pepper
1 large egg
¼ cup (60 g) heavy cream

MAKES 6 SERVING

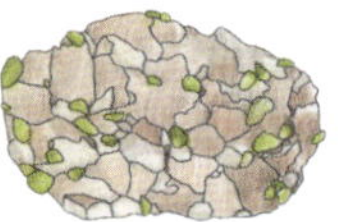

Using a knife, remove the rind and any bones from the pork belly, making sure to keep the fat on the belly (see Workshop, p. 21). Chop the pork belly into approximately ¼-inch (7mm) pieces (see Workshop, p. 21).

Remove the skin from the duck breast, and cut the breast into roughly ½-inch (1 ½ cm) cubes (see Workshop, p. 51).

Halve the pistachios.

Place the pork belly in a mixing bowl. Add the salt and pepper, mixing by hand (see Workshop, p. 21) or in a mixer on low speed. Add the halved pistachios.

Pour the egg and cream into the bowl and mix until uniform. Vigorously mix by hand or with a mixer on low speed for 5 minutes. Transfer the mixture to a mold and press firmly.

Place the mold in a cold oven. Set the temperature to 320°F (160°C) and bake using the convection setting (if possible) for 1 hour 30 minutes.

Remove the mold, and while still hot, use a paper towel to dab away any imperfections on the terrine's edges. Let it rest for 1 hour at room temperature, then refrigerate overnight. Remove from the refrigerator 30 minutes before serving.

Refrigerated leftovers will keep for 4 days.

PIES & TORTES

MAKING PUFF PASTRY

◆ ◆ ◆

For the ambitious, eager to embark on crafting flaky layers, this recipe stands as one of the simplest in its class. The folding steps demand meticulous attention, but ensure an exquisite puff pastry result.

WORKSHOP: PUFF PASTRY

4 cups (500 g) all-purpose flour | 1 ¾ cups (400 g) unsalted butter, chilled | 1 teaspoon salt | ⅔ cup (158 g) ice water

STEP 1

Cut the butter into ½-inch (1 ¼-cm) cubes.

STEP 2

In a large mixing bowl, combine the flour and salt.

STEP 3

Gradually incorporate the butter cubes into the flour mixture with your fingertips.

STEP 4

When the butter is still in large pieces, gradually add the ice water. Continue mixing until all the water has been added and a shaggy dough comes together.

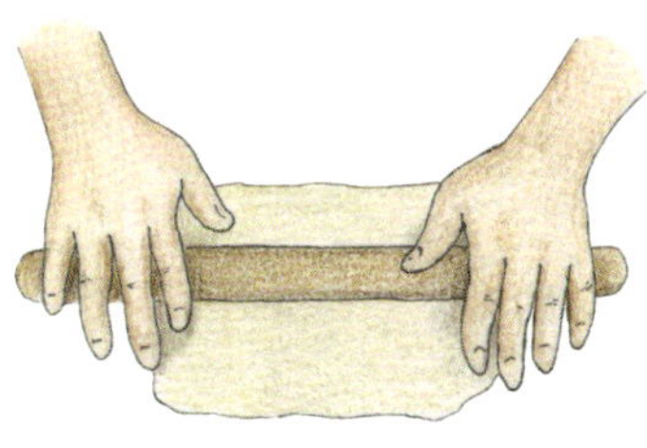

STEP 5

On a large piece of parchment paper, roll out the dough into a ¾-inch (2-cm) thick rectangle. Refrigerate for 30 minutes. Remove from the refrigerator and roll out the dough further into a 6- x 18-inch (15- x 45-cm) rectangle.

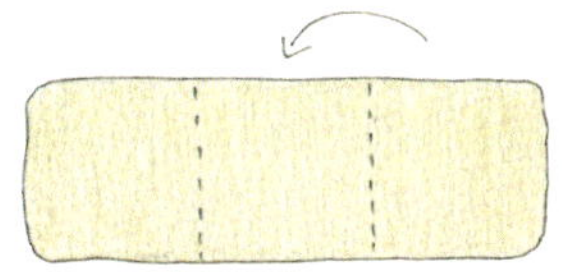

STEP 6

Fold one-third of the rectangle over the middle third and fold the final third over the previous two, aligning the edges.

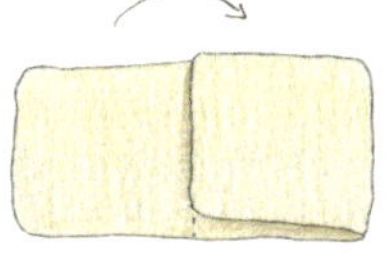

STEP 7

Turn the dough a quarter turn, roll it out as in Step 5, and repeat Step 6.

STEP 8

Turn the dough another quarter turn, roll, and repeat Step 6.

Wrap the dough in plastic wrap and chill in the refrigerator for at least 30 minutes before use.

ASSEMBLING A PIE OR TORTE

◆ ◆ ◆

Mastering the sealing technique for a pie or torte is crucial, not only to prevent the filling from escaping during baking, but also to achieve a beautiful, crisp, and golden appearance. A few tricks will ensure the dough is perfectly sealed.

WORKSHOP: ASSEMBLING TORTES & PIES

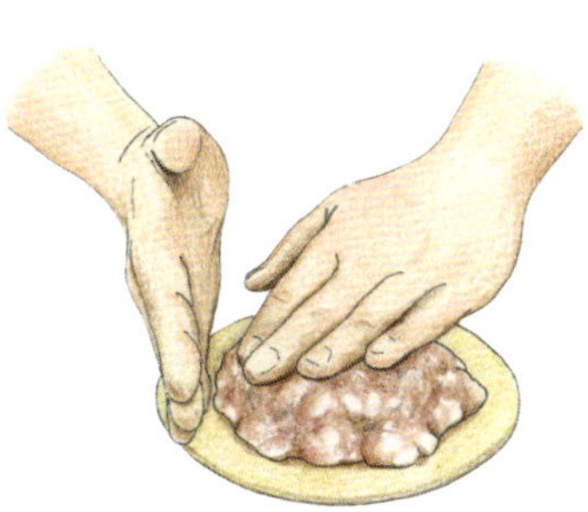

STEP 1

Spread the entire filling evenly on a rolled-out circle of dough, leaving uncovered dough at the edges.

STEP 2

With a pastry brush, apply a thin layer of beaten egg along the dough's uncovered edges.

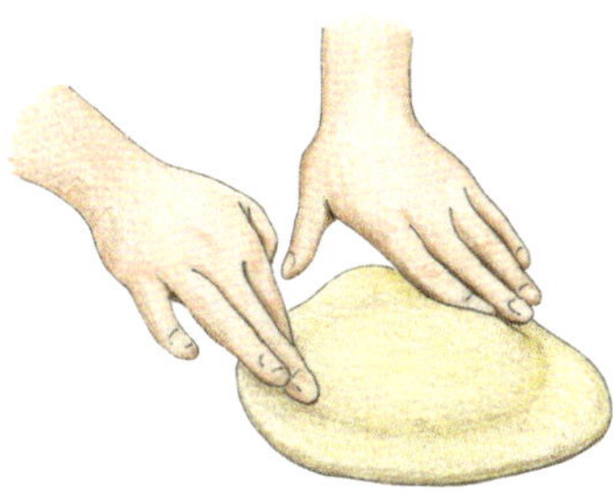

STEP 3

Cover the filling with the remaining rolled-out round of dough, matching the edges.

STEP 4

Trim about ¾ inch (2 cm) of excess dough from around the edges.

STEP 5

Press lightly around the edges with your fingertips to seal the dough.

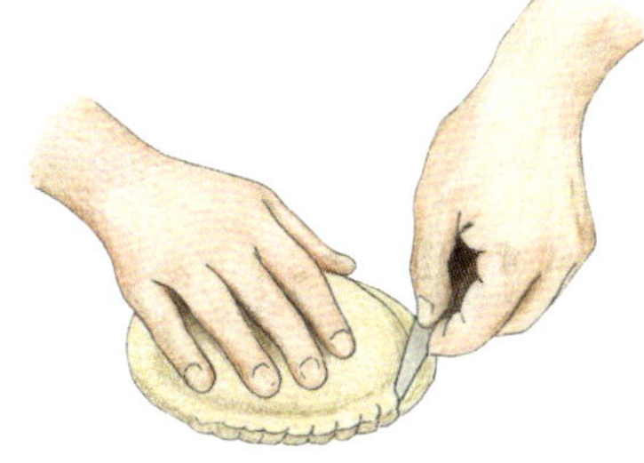

STEP 6

Mark the torte's edge with decorative grooves by gently pressing with the back of a knife.

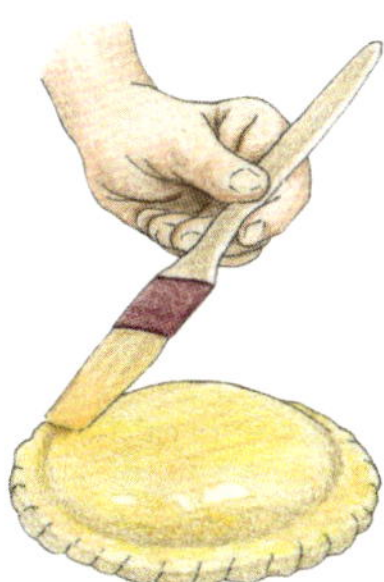

STEP 7

Brush the torte with the remaining beaten egg for a beautiful golden color.

STEP 8

Decorate the torte using the back of a knife, being careful not to press too hard.

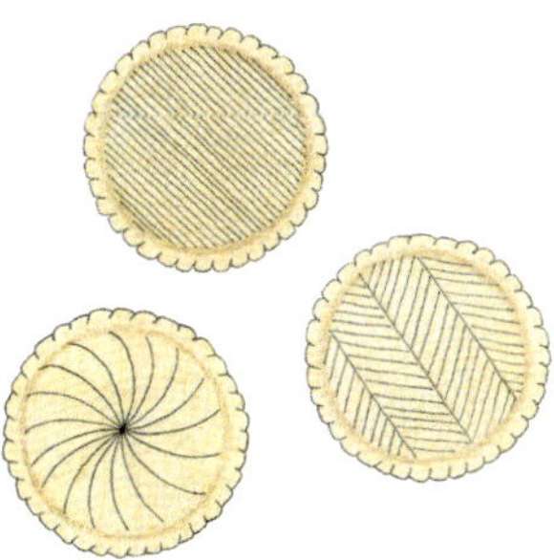

STEP 9

Try various designs and patterns, drawing inspiration as you see fit.

PREPARATION TIME
45 minutes

COOKING TIME
30 minutes

RESTING TIME
30 minutes

TORTES

HAM IN PUFF PASTRY

◆ ◆ ◆

INGREDIENTS

2 cups (515 g) whole milk
3 ½ tablespoons unsalted butter
¼ cup (50 g) all-purpose flour
1 teaspoon salt
2 pinches freshly ground pepper
½ batch (approx. 1 pound/500g) puff pastry (recipe p. 83)
6 medium slices ham
1 cup (150 g) grated Emmental cheese
2 large eggs

MAKES 6 SERVINGS

In a small saucepan, heat the milk until almost boiling and then remove it from the heat. In a separate medium saucepan, melt the butter, then gradually add the flour, stirring constantly, until you achieve a thick puree. Slowly pour in the hot milk, adding salt and pepper while stirring, to create a béchamel sauce. Refrigerate the sauce for 30 minutes.

Preheat the oven to 350°F (180 °C) using the convection setting (if possible). Divide the puff pastry in half and, using a rolling pin, roll each half out into an approximately 8-inch (20-cm) round. Line a baking sheet with parchment paper and place one round of pastry onto it. Lay one slice of ham in the center of the pastry, leaving at least 1 inch (2 ½ cm) of pastry exposed around the edges (see Workshop, p. 85). Layer with béchamel, followed by Emmental. Repeat the layering process—ham, béchamel, Emmental—until all ingredients have been used up.

In a bowl, beat the eggs. Brush the exposed pastry edges with a thin layer of the beaten egg (see Workshop, p. 85). Place the second round of pastry over the filling, pressing gently around the egg-washed area to seal (see Workshop, p. 85). Trim away the excess, up to about ¾ inch (2 cm), then press again to secure the seal.

Brush the pastry with the remaining beaten eggs and decorate the top of the dough if desired.

Bake for 30 minutes. Serve immediately.

PREPARATION TIME
45 minutes

COOKING TIME
30 minutes

ITALIAN-STYLE PUFF PASTRY

◆ ◆ ◆

INGREDIENTS

4 medium vine tomatoes
1 pinch salt
1 pinch freshly ground pepper
14 ounces (400 g) fresh mozzarella
½ batch (approx. 1 pound/500 g) puff pastry (recipe p. 83)
3 ½ ounces (100 g) medium slices Parma ham
2 large eggs

MAKES 6 SERVINGS

Cut the tomatoes into medium-thick slices and season with the salt and pepper. Slice the mozzarella slightly thinner than the tomato slices.

Preheat the oven to 350°F (180 °C) using the convection setting (if possible). Divide the puff pastry in half and, using a rolling pin, roll each half out into a rectangle. Line a baking sheet with parchment paper and place one rectangle of pastry onto it. Layer the ham on the pastry, leaving at least 1 inch (2 ½ cm) of pastry exposed around the edges (see Workshop, p. 85). Layer the tomatoes over the ham, then top with the slices of mozzarella.

In a bowl, beat the eggs. Brush the exposed pastry edges with a thin layer of the beaten egg (see Workshop, p. 85). Place the second rectangle of pastry over the filling, pressing gently around the egg-washed area to seal (see Workshop, p. 85). Trim away the excess, up to about ¾ inch (2 cm), then press again to secure the seal.

Brush the pastry with the remaining beaten eggs and decorate the top of the dough if desired.

Bake for 30 minutes. Serve immediately.

PREPARATION TIME
45 minutes

COOKING TIME
30 minutes

TORTES

FILET MIGNON PITHIVIER

INGREDIENTS

2 tablespoons unsalted butter, divided
1 pound (500 g) filet mignon
3 pinches salt
3 pinches freshly ground pepper
1 shallot
5 sprigs parsley
5 ½ ounces (150 g) white button mushrooms
½ batch (approx. 1 pound/500 g) puff pastry (recipe p. 83)
2 large eggs

MAKES 6 SERVINGS

In a small skillet over high heat, melt half the butter and briefly brown the filet mignon on all sides (do not cook through). Transfer to a plate and season with 2 pinches each of the salt and pepper.

Finely chop the shallot and parsley leaves. Dice the mushrooms.

In a medium skillet over medium heat, melt the remaining butter, then sauté the mushrooms and shallot for 2 minutes with 1 pinch each of the salt and pepper. Add parsley and stir for an additional minute.

Preheat the oven to 350°F (180 °C) using the convection setting (if possible). Divide the puff pastry in half and, using a rolling pin, roll each half out into a rectangle. Line a baking sheet with parchment paper and place one rectangle of pastry onto it.

Spread half of the mushroom, parsley, and shallot mixture on the pastry in the shape of the filet mignon, making sure to leave at least 1 inch (2 ½ cm) dough uncovered at the edges. Place the filet on top and cover with the remaining vegetable mixture.

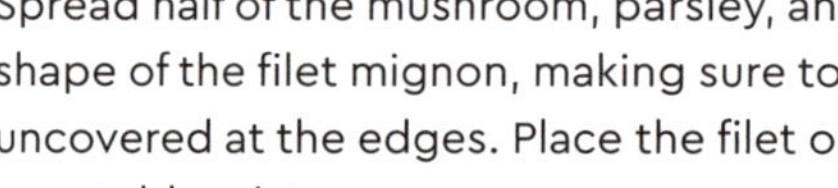

In a bowl, beat the eggs. Brush the exposed pastry edges with a thin layer of the beaten egg (see Workshop, p. 85). Place the second rectangle of pastry over the filling, pressing gently around the egg-washed area to seal (see Workshop, p. 85). Trim away the excess, up to about ¾ inch (2 cm), then press again to secure the seal.

Brush the pastry with the remaining beaten eggs and decorate the top of the dough if desired.

Bake for 30 minutes. Serve immediately.

PREPARATION TIME
1 hour

COOKING TIME
30 minutes

TORTES

HONEY CHICKEN PITHIVIER

◆ ◆ ◆

INGREDIENTS

1 medium zucchini
1 medium eggplant
Olive oil, for drizzling
3 pinches salt
3 pinches freshly ground pepper
2 heaping teaspoons honey
½ batch (approx. 1 pound/500 g) puff pastry (recipe p. 83)
1 pound (500 g) puff pastry (recipe p. 83)
2 large eggs

MAKES 6 SERVINGS

Cut the zucchini and eggplant into approximately ¼-inch (7-mm) dice.

In two medium skillets over medium heat, pour a drizzle of olive oil and cook the zucchini and eggplant separately until tender. Season each mixture with 1 pinch each of the salt and pepper. Once the vegetables are tender, add 1 heaping teaspoon of honey to each skillet and stir to combine.

Drain the vegetables on paper towels, then combine them in a bowl, and refrigerate until ready to use.

Wipe one skillet clean, add a drizzle of olive oil, and sear the chicken breast on high heat for approximately 20 seconds on each side, to color but not cook through. Season with 1 pinch each of the salt and pepper.

Preheat the oven to 350°F (180 °C) using the convection setting (if possible). Divide the puff pastry in half and, using a rolling pin, roll each half out into a rectangle. Line a baking sheet with parchment paper and place one rectangle of pastry onto it.

Spread half of the vegetable mixture onto the pastry, making sure to leave at least 1 inch (2 ½ cm) uncovered at the edges (see Workshop, p. 85). Place the chicken on top and cover with the remaining vegetable mixture.

In a bowl, beat the eggs. Brush the exposed pastry edges with a thin layer of the beaten egg (see Workshop, p. 85). Place the second rectangle of pastry over the filling, pressing gently around the egg-washed area to seal (see Workshop, p. 85). Trim away the excess, up to about ¾ inch (2 cm), then press again to secure the seal.

Brush the pastry with the remaining beaten eggs and decorate the top of the dough if desired. Bake for 30 minutes. Serve immediately.

PREPARATION TIME
40 minutes

COOKING TIME
30 minutes + 30 minutes

TORTES

BLUE CHEESE, PEAR, & PORK TORTE

◆ ◆ ◆

INGREDIENTS

2 pears
1 ½ pounds (750 g) boneless pork shoulder
2 teaspoons salt
2 pinches freshly ground pepper
3 large eggs, divided
3 tablespoons heavy cream
9 ounces (250 g) Fourme d'Ambert or other blue cheese
½ batch (approx. 1 pound/500 g) puff pastry (recipe p. 83)

MAKES 6 SERVINGS

Place the pears in a cold oven set to 320°F (160°C) for 30 minutes. Remove from the oven and set aside. Set the oven temperature to 350°F (180°C) using the convection setting (if possible).

Cut the pork shoulder into ½-inch (1 ¼-cm) cubes. Place in a mixing bowl, add the salt and pepper and vigorously mix by hand or with a mixer on low speed for 5 minutes. Pour one egg and the cream into the bowl and mix until uniform.

Peel, core, and quarter the baked pears. Cut the pear quarters into ½-inch (1 ¼-cm) cubes and fold them into the pork mixture until combined evenly. Slice the blue cheese into thick, even pieces.

Divide the puff pastry in half and, using a rolling pin, roll each half out into an 8-inch (20-cm) round. Line a baking sheet with parchment paper and place one round of pastry onto it. Spread the pear and pork mixture in a circle, leaving at least 1 inch (2 ½ cm) of pastry exposed around the edges (see Workshop, p. 85). Layer the cheese evenly over the filling.

In a bowl, beat the remaining 2 eggs. Brush the exposed pastry edges with a thin layer of the beaten egg (see Workshop, p. 85). Place the second round of pastry over the filling, pressing gently around the egg-washed area to seal (see Workshop, p. 85). Trim away the excess, up to about ¾ inch (2 cm), then press again to secure the seal.

Brush the pastry with the remaining beaten eggs and decorate the top of the dough if desired.

Bake for 30 minutes. Serve immediately.

PREPARATION TIME
1 hour 30 minutes

COOKING TIME
30 minutes

TORTES

HOLIDAY PORK & CHICKEN TORTE

◆ ◆ ◆

INGREDIENTS

1 pound (500 g) whole pork belly or 1 pound (500 g) minced pork belly
1 pound (500 g) boneless skinless chicken breast
3 teaspoons salt
3 pinches freshly ground pepper
3 large eggs, divided
3 tablespoons heavy cream
½ batch (approx. 1 pound/500 g) puff pastry (recipe p. 83)

MAKES 6 SERVINGS

Using a knife, remove the rind and any bones from the pork belly, making sure to keep the fat on the belly (see Workshop, p. 21).

Cube the pork belly into approximately ½-inch (1 ½ cm) pieces (see Workshop, p. 51). Set aside.

Cut the chicken breast into approximately ½-inch (1 ½ cm) cubes. Transfer to a bowl and refrigerate.

Place the pork belly in a mixing bowl, add the salt and pepper, and vigorously mix by hand or with a mixer on low speed for 5 minutes. Pour 1 egg and the cream into the bowl and mix until uniform. Add the chicken, mixing either by hand or in a mixer on low speed for 5 minutes.

Divide the puff pastry in half and, using a rolling pin, roll each half out into an 8-inch (20-cm) round. Line a baking sheet with parchment paper and place one round of pastry onto it. Spread the filling mixture in a circle, leaving at least 1 inch (2 ½ cm) of pastry exposed around the edges (see Workshop, p. 85).

In a bowl, beat the remaining 2 eggs. Brush the exposed pastry edges with a thin layer of the beaten egg (see Workshop, p. 85). Place the second round of pastry over the filling, pressing gently around the egg-washed area to seal (see Workshop, p. 85). Trim away the excess, up to about ¾ inch (2 cm), then press again to secure the seal.

Brush the pastry with the remaining beaten eggs and decorate the top of the dough if desired.

Place the tray in a cold oven, set the temperature to 350°F (180°C), and bake using the convection setting (if possible) for 30 minutes. Serve immediately.

PREPARATION TIME
1 hour

COOKING TIME
30 minutes

SAVOYARD TORTE

◆ ◆ ◆

INGREDIENTS

½ pound (250 g) small potatoes
1 full round (approx. 7-8 inches/500 g) Reblochon or Brie cheese
½ batch (approx. 1 pound/500 g) puff pastry (recipe p. 83)
2 large eggs
2 pinches salt
1 pinch freshly ground pepper

MAKES 6 SERVINGS

Boil the potatoes until tender (they should be easily pierced with a knife). Once cooked, peel and slice them into ½-inch (1 ½ cm) rounds and season with salt and pepper.

Slice the Reblochon or Brie round in half horizontally to yield two equal-sized discs.

Preheat the oven to 350°F (180 °C) using the convection setting (if possible).

Divide the puff pastry in half and, using a rolling pin, roll each half out into an 8-inch (20-cm) round. Line a baking sheet with parchment paper and place one round of pastry onto it. Set one disc of cheese in the center of the pastry, leaving at least 1 inch (2 ½ cm) of pastry exposed around the edges (see Workshop, p. 85). Cover with potato slices, then add the second disc of cheese on top.

In a bowl, beat the eggs. Brush the exposed pastry edges with a thin layer of the beaten egg (see Workshop, p. 85). Place the second round of pastry over the filling, pressing gently around the egg-washed area to seal (see Workshop, p. 85). Trim away the excess, up to about ¾ inch (2 cm), then press again to secure the seal.

Brush the pastry with the remaining beaten eggs and decorate the top of the dough if desired.

Bake for 30 minutes. Serve immediately.

PREPARATION TIME
1 hour

COOKING TIME
30 minutes

TORTES

PROVENÇAL PORK TORTE

◆ ◆ ◆

INGREDIENTS

1 pound (500 g) whole pork belly or 1 pound (500 g) minced pork belly
1 pound (500 g) boneless pork shoulder or ¾ pounds (300 g) minced pork shoulder
3 teaspoons salt
2 pinches freshly ground pepper
3 teaspoons herbes de Provence
3 large eggs, divided
¼ cup (60 g) heavy cream
½ batch (approx. 1 pound/500 g) puff pastry (recipe p. 83)

6 PERSONNES

Using a knife, remove the rind and any bones from the pork belly, making sure to keep the fat on the belly (see Workshop, p. 21).

Cube the pork belly into approximately ½-inch (1 ½ cm) pieces (see Workshop, p. 51). Set aside.

Cut the pork shoulder into approximately ½-inch (1 ½ cm) cubes.

Place the diced pork belly in a mixing bowl, and add the salt, pepper, and herbes de Provence. Mix either by hand (see Workshop, p. 21) or with a mixer on low speed.

Add 1 egg and the cream to the bowl, and mix until well combined. Add the pork shoulder and vigorously mix by hand or with a mixer on low speed for 5 minutes. Preheat the oven to 350°F (180 °C) using the convection setting (if possible).

Divide the puff pastry in half and, using a rolling pin, roll each half out into an 8-inch (20-cm) round. Line a baking sheet with parchment paper and place one round of pastry onto it. Spread the pork mixture in a circle on the pastry, leaving at least 1 inch (2 ½ cm) of pastry exposed around the edges (see Workshop, p. 85).

In a bowl, beat the remaining 2 eggs. Brush the exposed pastry edges with a thin layer of the beaten egg (see Workshop, p. 85). Place the second round of pastry over the filling, pressing gently around the egg-washed area to seal (see Workshop, p. 85). Trim away the excess, up to about ¾ inch (2 cm), then press again to secure the seal.

Brush the pastry with the remaining beaten eggs and decorate the top of the dough if desired. Bake for 30 minutes. Serve immediately.

PREPARATION TIME
1 hour

COOKING TIME
40 minutes

TORTES

PIPERADE-INSPIRED TORTE

◆ ◆ ◆

INGREDIENTS

1 yellow onion
2 garlic cloves
1 red bell pepper
1 green bell pepper
2 medium tomatoes
Olive oil, for drizzling
1 teaspoon salt
2 pinches freshly ground pepper
1 pinch ground Espelette pepper
4 large eggs, divided
3 ½ ounces (100 g) cured ham
½ batch (approx. 1 pound/500 g) puff pastry (recipe p. 83)

MAKES 6 SERVINGS

Finely chop the onion. Press the garlic cloves with the flat side of a knife to remove the peel and then finely chop the garlic.

Slice the bell peppers into thin strips, discarding the seeds and white membranes. Cut the tomatoes into eighths, removing the stem and seeds to retain only the flesh.

In a medium skillet over medium heat, sauté the onion in a drizzle of olive oil. Add the bell peppers and cook for 10 minutes. Add the tomatoes and continue cooking for 5 minutes. Season with the salt, pepper, and Espelette pepper. Add 2 of the eggs and the garlic and mix vigorously for 2 minutes. Adjust the seasoning if necessary.

Cut the ham into thin strips.

Preheat the oven to 350°F (180 °C) using the convection setting (if possible).

Divide the puff pastry in half and, using a rolling pin, roll each half out into an 8-inch (20-cm) round. Line a baking sheet with parchment paper and place one round of pastry onto it. Spread the vegetable mixture in a circle on the pastry, leaving at least 1 inch (2 ½ cm) of pastry exposed around the edges (see Workshop, p. 85). Layer the ham on top.

In a bowl, beat the remaining 2 eggs. Brush the exposed pastry edges with a thin layer of the beaten egg (see Workshop, p. 85). Place the second round of pastry over the filling, pressing gently around the egg-washed area to seal (see Workshop, p. 85). Trim away the excess, up to about ¾ inch (2 cm), then press again to secure the seal.

Brush the pastry with the remaining beaten eggs and decorate the top of the dough if desired. Bake for 40 minutes. Serve immediately.

PREPARATION TIME
1 hour (30 minutes initial prep, 30 minutes before baking)

COOKING TIME
30 minutes

RESTING TIME
8 hours (up to 24 hours recommended)

TORTES

PÂTÉ LORRAIN

◆ ◆ ◆

INGREDIENTS

10 ½ ounces (300 g) boneless veal shoulder
10 ½ ounces (300 g) boneless pork shoulder
1 ½ shallots
½ bunch parsley
2 teaspoons salt
1 pinch freshly ground pepper
½ cup (120 g) white wine
½ batch (approx. 1 pound/500 g) puff pastry (recipe p. 83)
2 large eggs

MAKES 6 SERVINGS

The Night Before:

Cube the veal and pork into ½-inch (1 ½-cm) cubes (see Workshop, p. 51). Finely chop the shallots and parsley leaves.

In a mixing bowl, combine the veal, pork, salt, and pepper. Add the chopped shallots and parsley. Mix well, and pour in the white wine, stirring to combine.

Cover the mixture with plastic wrap, pressing it directly against the surface to prevent air exposure. Let it marinate for at least 8 hours in the refrigerator, and up to 24 hours for the best flavor.

The Day of:

Remove the marinated mixture from the refrigerator, pour into a strainer, and let drain for 15 minutes.

Preheat the oven to 350°F (180 °C) using the convection setting (if possible). Divide the puff pastry in half and, using a rolling pin, roll each half out into a rectangle. Line a baking sheet with parchment paper and place one rectangle of pastry onto it.

Spread the marinated mixture onto the pastry, making sure to leave at least 1 inch (2 ½ cm) uncovered at the edges (see Workshop, p. 85).

In a bowl, beat the eggs. Brush the exposed pastry edges with a thin layer of the beaten egg (see Workshop, p. 85). Place the second rectangle of pastry over the filling, pressing gently around the egg-washed area to seal (see Workshop, p. 85). Trim away the excess, up to about ¾ inch (2 cm), then press again to secure the seal.

Brush the pastry with the remaining beaten eggs and decorate the top of the dough if desired.

Bake for 30 minutes. Serve immediately.

RILLETTES

SHREDDING & MIXING RILLETTES

◆ ◆ ◆

Achieving perfect rillettes is all about slow cooking. Meat should simmer for hours to achieve that melt-in-the-mouth texture. The final shredding process is also crucial and should be done with the utmost care.

WORKSHOP: SHREDDING MEAT

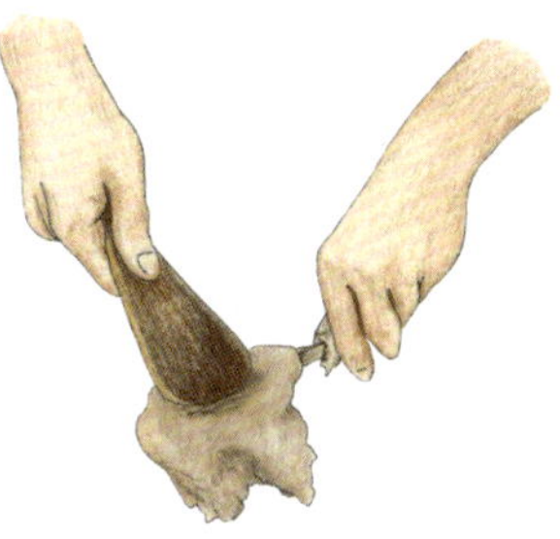

STEP 1

Once cooked, press the meat using a wooden spatula. It should shred upon contact.

STEP 2

Carefully shred the meat further with your fingers to obtain fine pieces.

MIXING STEP BY STEP

STEP 1

Mix the shredded meat with fat that's been melted over medium heat in a saucepan.

STEP 2

Using a spatula, stir to combine the fat and meat.

PREPARATION TIME
50 minutes

COOKING TIME
4 hours

RESTING TIME
8 hours

RILLETTES

LE MANS-STYLE RILLETTES

◆ ◆ ◆

INGREDIENTS

2 ¼ pounds (1 kg) boneless pork shoulder
2 ¼ cups (500 g) lard
6 teaspoons salt
6 pinches freshly ground pepper

MAKES 6 SERVINGS

Cut the pork shoulder into 1 ¼-inch (3-cm) cubes.

Melt the lard in a medium pot over medium heat. Reduce the heat to maintain a gentle simmer, add the pork cubes, and cook, covered, for 2 hours, turning the meat every hour. Stir in the salt and pepper and then cook for an additional 2 hours, turning the meat every hour until it shreds at the touch of a spatula.

Set a strainer over a medium bowl and pour the contents of the pot into the strainer, collecting the fat in the bowl. Remove the pork cubes to a separate container.

Shred the pork by hand, then add three-quarters of the reserved fat to it, mixing well (see Workshop, p. 109).

Cover and refrigerate the mixture, stirring every 15 minutes for 1 hour 30 minutes to achieve a consistent texture. Continue to refrigerate it for 8 hours. Remove from the refrigerator 30 minutes before serving.

Refrigerated leftovers will keep for 4 days.

PALLARES
SOLSONA

PREPARATION TIME
50 minutes

COOKING TIME
3 hours

RESTING TIME
4 hours

RILLETTES

MUSTARD RABBIT RILLETTES

◆ ◆ ◆

INGREDIENTS

1 medium carrot
2 yellow onions, divided
6 ¼ cups (1.5 liters) water
2 bunches parsley, divided
4 teaspoons salt
3 pinches freshly ground pepper
3 heads garlic
3 ¼ pounds (1.5 kg) rabbit thighs
1 bunch tarragon
¼ cup plus 3 tablespoons (100 g) grainy mustard
Olive oil, for drizzling

MAKES 6 SERVINGS

Chop the carrot into 6 pieces and roughly chop 1 onion. Fill a large pot with the water and add the carrot, onion, 1 bunch of the parsley, and the salt and pepper. Bring to a boil and then reduce the heat and simmer for 30 minutes.

While the vegetables simmer, place the garlic heads on a baking sheet and place in a cold oven. Set the temperature to 355°F (180°C) and bake for 30 minutes. Remove and set aside to cool.

Add the rabbit thighs into the pot, making sure that everything is submerged. Continue to simmer for approximately 2 hours. The rabbit is done when a fork pierces the meat effortlessly. Remove the rabbit from the pot and cool to room temperature. Discard the cooked vegetables.

While the rabbit simmers, peel the roasted garlic, halve the cloves, remove the germ if needed, and mash to form a paste.

Coarsely chop the tarragon and remaining parsley leaves. Thinly slice the remaining onion.

Debone the rabbit thighs, shred by hand, and transfer to a bowl (see Workshop, p. 109). Add the grainy mustard, followed by a drizzle of olive oil, the garlic paste, chopped herbs, and onion slices and mix well.

Chill for 4 hours in the refrigerator. Remove 30 minutes prior to serving. Refrigerated leftovers will keep for 4 days.

PREPARATION TIME
50 minutes

COOKING TIME
4 hours 35 minutes

RESTING TIME
8 hours

RILLETTES

TRADITIONAL TOURS RILLETTES

◆ ◆ ◆

INGREDIENTS

2 ¼ pounds (1 kg) boneless pork shoulder
1 pound (500 g) lard
6 teaspoons salt
6 pinches freshly ground pepper

MAKES 6 SERVINGS

Cut the pork shoulder into 1-inch (2 ½-cm) cubes.

Melt the lard in a medium pot over high heat. Add the pork cubes and stir for about 20 minutes until all sides have a deep brown color.

Reduce the heat to maintain a gentle simmer and cook the pork, covered, for 2 hours, turning the meat every hour. Stir in the salt and pepper and then cook for an additional 2 hours, turning the meat every hour until it shreds at the touch of a spatula.

Remove the pork from the pot and shred it by hand (see Workshop, p. 109).

Once shredded, return the pork to the pot and cook over high heat for about 15 minutes, stirring continuously to give it a rich color. Transfer the shredded meat, along with half of its fat, to a bowl.

Cover and refrigerate the mixture, stirring every 15 minutes for 1 hour 30 minutes to achieve a consistent texture. Continue to refrigerate for 8 hours. Remove from the refrigerator 30 minutes before serving.

Refrigerated leftovers will keep for 4 days.

PREPARATION TIME
30 minutes

COOKING TIME
4 hours

RESTING TIME
8 hours

RILLETTES

DUCK & PORK RILLETTES

◆ ◆ ◆

INGREDIENTS

1 pound (500 g) boneless pork shoulder
1 pound (500 g) duck fat
3 duck legs
6 teaspoons fine salt
6 pinches freshly ground pepper

MAKES 6 SERVINGS

Cut the pork shoulder into 1 ½-inch (3 ½-cm) cubes.

In a large pot over medium heat, melt the duck fat.

Reduce the heat to maintain a gentle simmer. Add the duck and pork, and cook, covered, for 2 hours, turning the pieces every hour. Stir in the salt and pepper and stir then cook for an additional 2 hours, turning the meat every hour until it shreds at the touch of a spatula.

Set a strainer over a medium bowl and pour the contents of the pot into the strainer, collecting the fat in the bowl. Remove the meat to a separate container.

Remove the skin and bones from the duck.

Shred the duck and pork by hand (see Workshop, p. 109) and transfer the meat to a bowl. Mix in one ladle of fat, and let it sit for 15 minutes.

Repeat the process until half of the fat has been incorporated (you can use the remaining fat for other cooking needs, such as frying sausages or meatballs).

Cover and refrigerate the mixture, stirring every 15 minutes for 1 hour 30 minutes to achieve a consistent texture. Continue to refrigerate for 8 hours. Remove from the refrigerator 30 minutes before serving.

Refrigerated leftovers will keep for 4 days.

PREPARATION TIME
30 minutes

COOKING TIME
4 hours

RESTING TIME
8 hours

RILLETTES

GOOSE & PORK RILLETTES

◆ ◆ ◆

INGREDIENTS

4 confit goose legs
1 pound (500 g) goose fat
1 pound (500 g) boneless pork shoulder
6 teaspoons salt
6 pinches freshly ground pepper

MAKES 6 SERVINGS

Cut the pork shoulder into approximately 1 ½-inch (3 ½-cm) cubes. In a large pot over medium heat, melt the goose fat.

Add the pork to the pot; reduce heat to a gentle simmer and cook, covered, for 2 hours.

Add the confit goose legs and the salt and pepper and cook for an additional 2 hours or more, stirring occasionally until the meat shreds upon contact with a spatula.

Set a strainer over a medium bowl and pour the contents of the pot into the strainer, collecting the fat in the bowl. Remove the meat to a separate container. Remove the skin and bones from the goose.

Shred the goose and pork by hand (see Workshop, p. 109) and transfer the meat to a bowl. Mix in one ladle of fat, and let it sit for 15 minutes.

Repeat the process until half the fat has been incorporated (you can use the remaining fat for other cooking needs, such as frying sausages or meatballs).

Cover and refrigerate the mixture, stirring every 15 minutes for 1 hour 30 minutes to achieve a consistent texture. Continue to refrigerate for 8 hours. Remove from the refrigerator 30 minutes before serving.

Refrigerated leftovers will keep for 4 days.

PREPARATION TIME	COOKING TIME	RESTING TIME
1 hour	4 hours 30 minutes	4 hours

RILLETTES

BÁNH MÌ-INSPIRED RILLETTES

◆ ◆ ◆

INGREDIENTS

10 ½ cups (2 ½ liters) water
2 bunches cilantro, divided
4 teaspoons plus 1 pinch salt, divided
4 pinches freshly ground pepper
1 yellow onion
2 medium carrots, divided
2 medium zucchini
Olive oil, for drizzling
2 heads garlic
1 pound (500 g) pork belly
2 chicken thighs
½ cucumber
2 tablespoons nước mắm
3 tablespoons soy sauce

MAKES 6 SERVINGS

In a large pot, pour in the water and add 1 ½ bunches of the cilantro, 4 teaspoons of the salt and 3 pinches of the pepper. Chop the onion and 1 ½ of the carrots into large cubes and add them to the pot. Bring to a boil; reduce heat to a simmer and cook for 30 minutes. While vegetables simmer, halve the zucchinis lengthwise, sprinkle with the remaining 1 pinch each of salt and pepper, and drizzle with olive oil.

Place the garlic heads and zucchini on a baking sheet and place in a cold oven. Set the temperature to 320°F (160 °C) and bake for 45 minutes. Remove the garlic and continue cooking the zucchini for an additional 30 minutes. Scoop out the zucchini flesh ("zucchini caviar") and set aside, discarding the peel. Peel the roasted garlic, halve the cloves, remove the germ if needed, and mash to form a paste.

Add the pork (split into 2 pieces) and chicken thighs to the simmering pot. Top with additional water if necessary to fully submerge the meat. Continue simmering for roughly 3 hours 30 minutes, until a fork pierces the meat effortlessly. Remove the pork and chicken and cool to room temperature. Discard the vegetables and simmering water.

Slice the remaining ½ carrot lengthwise and then julienne it finely. Slice the cucumber lengthwise, remove the seeds, and then julienne it finely. Roughly chop the leaves from the remaining ½ bunch of cilantro.

Remove the skin and bones from both the pork and chicken. Shred the meats by hand (see Workshop, p. 109) and place in a large bowl. Stir in the nước mắm, soy sauce, garlic paste, and zucchini caviar. Add the carrots, cucumbers, and cilantro, and mix well.

Cover and refrigerate the mixture for 4 hours. Remove from the refrigerator 30 minutes before serving. Refrigerated leftovers will keep for 4 days.

STAUB
STAUB

PREPARATION TIME
1 hour

COOKING TIME
2 hours 30 minutes

RESTING TIME
4 hours

RILLETTES

CHICKEN RILLETTES WITH TAPENADE

◆ ◆ ◆

INGREDIENTS

10 ½ cups (2 ½ l) water
1 bunch parsley
1 yellow onion
1 medium carrot
4 teaspoons salt
3 pinches freshly ground pepper
1 garlic clove
7 ounces (200 g) pitted black olives
5 anchovies
9 capers
5 tablespoons olive oil, divided
2 ¼ pounds (1 kg) bone-in chicken thighs

MAKES 6 SERVINGS

In a large pot, pour in the water and add the parsley, salt, and pepper. Cut the onion and carrot into rough cubes and add them to the pot. Bring to a boil; reduce heat to a simmer and cook for 30 minutes.

While vegetables simmer, peel the garlic, remove the germ, and mince.

Coarsly chop the olives, anchovies, capers and garlic then combine them in a small bowl. Add 3 tablespoons of the olive oil and stir to bind the ingredients into a tapenade. Set aside.

Add the chicken thighs to the pot. Top with additional water if necessary to fully submerge the meat. Simmer for 2 hours, until a fork easily pierces the chicken and the meat separates from the bone. Remove chicken pieces from the water and cool to room temperature. Discard water and vegetables.

Once cooled, remove the skin and bones from the chicken, shred the meat by hand (see Workshop, p. 109), and place it in a mixing bowl.

Stir the tapenade into to the chicken, compacting the mixture with your fist to achieve a spreadable texture. Add the remaining 2 tablespoons of olive oil and mix thoroughly. Adjust seasoning if needed.

Cover and refrigerate for 4 hours. Remove from the refrigerator 30 minutes before serving.

Refrigerated leftovers will keep for 3 days.

PREPARATION TIME
1 hour

COOKING TIME
1 hour

RESTING TIME
4 hours

RILLETTES

VEGETABLE RILLETTES

◆ ◆ ◆

INGREDIENTS

3 medium zucchini
2 medium eggplants
Olive oil, for drizzling
1 pinch salt
1 pinch freshly ground pepper
4 medium tomatoes
1 bunch spring onions or 2 bunches green onions
1 bell pepper
1 bunch cilantro

MAKES 6 SERVINGS

Halve the zucchini and cut the eggplants lengthwise into eighths. Place them on a baking sheet, drizzle with olive oil, and season with 1 pinch each of salt and pepper.

Remove the stems from the tomatoes, quarter them, discard the seeds and juice, retaining only the flesh. Add them to the baking sheet.

Trim the onions, reserving half. Quarter the bell pepper, removing seeds and membranes, and add the onions and pepper to the baking sheet.

Place the baking sheet in a cold oven, set the temperature to 320°F (160°C), and bake for 15 minutes. Remove the tomatoes from the tray and set aside to cool. Bake the remaining vegetables for 30 more minutes, then remove the bell pepper and onions. Bake the eggplant and zucchini for 30 more minutes.

Peel the skins off the tomatoes and bell pepper.

Use a teaspoon to scoop out the flesh from the zucchini and eggplants, then mash them in a mixing bowl with a fork.

Thinly slice the cooked tomatoes and bell pepper, and the remaining raw onions. Roughly chop the cilantro. In a large bowl, combine all ingredients and mix thoroughly. Adjust seasonings as necessary and add any more olive oil desired, then stir well.

Cover and refrigerate for 4 hours. Remove from the refrigerator 30 minutes before serving.

Refrigerated leftovers will keep for 3 days.

STAUB
STAUB

PREPARATION TIME
1 hour

COOKING TIME
2 hours 30 minutes

RESTING TIME
4 hours

RILLETTES

TARRAGON CHICKEN RILLETTES

◆ ◆ ◆

INGREDIENTS

10 ½ cups (2 ½ l) water
1 bunch parsley
1 head garlic
6 teaspoons salt
6 pinches freshly ground pepper
1 yellow onion
1 medium carrot
2 ¼ pounds (1 kg) bone-in chicken thighs
2 eggplants
5 tablespoons olive oil, plus more for drizzling
1 bunch tarragon

MAKES 6 SERVINGS

In a large pot, pour in the water and add the parsley, garlic, salt, and pepper. Cut the onion and carrot into rough cubes and add them to the pot. Bring to a boil; reduce heat to a simmer and cook for 30 minutes.

Add the chicken thighs to the pot, ensuring they are fully submerged. Simmer until the chicken can be easily pierced with a fork, about 2 hours. Remove the chicken from the pot and cool to room temperature. Discard water and vegetables.

While chicken cooks, cut the eggplant lengthwise into eight pieces. Place on a baking sheet, drizzle with olive oil, season with salt and pepper, and place in a cold oven set to 350°F (180°C) for 30 minutes. The eggplant is ready when its flesh can easily be separated from the skin with a spoon. Mash the eggplant flesh to achieve an eggplant caviar consistency.

Remove the tarragon leaves from the stems and coarsly chop the leaves.

Remove the skin and bones from the chicken, then shred the meat by hand (see Workshop, p. 109) and place in a mixing bowl. Add the eggplant and tarragon and stir to combine, then press down with your fist to achieve the spreadable texture.

Add 5 tablespoons of olive oil and mix thoroughly. Adjust seasonings as necessary.

Cover and refrigerate for 4 hours. Remove from the refrigerator 30 minutes before serving.

Refrigerated leftovers will keep for 3 days.

PREPARATION TIME
1 hour

COOKING TIME
4 hours 30 minutes

RESTING TIME
4 hours

RILLETTES

BEEF RILLETTES

◆ ◆ ◆

INGREDIENTS

10 ½ cups (2 ½ l) water
2 garlic cloves
2 bunches parsley, divided
6 teaspoons plus 2 pinches salt, divided
5 pinches freshly ground pepper
2 yellow onions
2 medium carrots, divided
1 pound (500 g) tomatoes
1 eggplant
Olive oil, for drizzling
1 bunch tarragon
2 ¼ pounds (1 kg) boneless beef short ribs
3 ½ ounces (100 g) cornichons
2 medium red onions
Vinegar (optional)

MAKES 6 SERVINGS

In a large pot, pour in the water and add the garlic, 1 ½ bunches of the parsley, 6 teaspoons of the salt, and 3 pinches of the pepper. Cut the yellow onions and 1 carrot into rough cubes and add them to the pot. Bring to a boil; reduce heat to a simmer and cook for 30 minutes.

While vegetables simmer, quarter the tomatoes, removing the stems and cores (reserve the cores), and place them on a baking sheet. Drizzle with olive oil and 1 pinch each of the salt and pepper. Add the tomato cores to the simmering pot.

Slice the eggplant lengthwise into eight pieces, drizzle with olive oil and 1 pinch each of the salt and pepper, and place next to the tomatoes on the baking sheet.

Place the tomatoes and eggplant in a cold oven set to 320°F (160°C). After 15 minutes, remove the tomatoes, then continue baking the eggplant for an additional 45 minutes. While they're still warm, peel the tomatoes. When eggplant is done, using a teaspoon, scoop out the eggplant flesh and set aside. Finely chop the tarragon leaves and remaining parsley leaves.

After the pot has been simmering for 30 minutes, add the beef, along with more water if necessary to ensure all ingredients are submerged. Simmer for about 4 hours. The beef is done when it can be easily pierced with a fork. Remove the beef from the water and let cool to room temperature. Shred the beef by hand (see Workshop, p. 109) and place in a large mixing bowl.

Halve the pickles lengthwise, then slice them into thin strips, about 1/16 inch (1 mm) wide. Cut the cooked tomato and raw red onions into thin slices like the pickles.

Add the tomatoes, red onions, pickles, eggplant caviar, tarragon, and chopped parsley to the beef. Mix well. Add olive oil and vinegar if desired, adjust seasonings if necessary, and mix again. Cover and refrigerate for 4 hours. Remove from the refrigerator 30 minutes before serving.

Refrigerated leftovers will keep for 3 days.

STAUB
STAUB

ALCOHOLS

SUBTLE AND AROMATIC

◆ ◆ ◆

Much like spices, wines and spirits, when delicately balanced, imbue terrines, pâtés, sausages, and foie gras with flavor. The alcohol should highlight other ingredients without overshadowing them. To maintain this balance, the amount of alcohol added to the preparation should not exceed 2% of its total weight.

PAIRING ALCOHOL WITH CHARCUTERIE: A FEW TIPS

ARMAGNAC

Originating from a southwestern French region encompassing much of Gers, southern Lot-et-Garonne, and eastern Landes, this brandy made from grapes is used similarly to cognac but is crafted in a more artisanal manner.

COGNAC

Cognac, a brandy made from white wine, primarily originates from the Charente region in southwestern France. It's cherished for lending character to foie gras as well as pâtés and terrines. Young, it emanates fruity notes, which evolve into floral, then woody, and finally spicy aromas and flavors as it ages.

MADEIRA

A Portuguese specialty from a volcanic island off the west coast of Morocco, Madeira is prevalent in charcuterie production. This sweet wine is used like port but has a more acidic taste.

PORT

A specialty from Haut-Douro, in northern Portugal, port is sweet, with a high alcohol content. Its blend of strength and smoothness complements traditional recipes like Grandma's Pâté (recipe p. 26) or the Country Pâté (recipe p. 22).

WINE

Wine is incorporated in many pâté, terrine, and sausage recipes. It imparts flavor, albeit with less intensity than other alcohols. Using a robust-tasting bottle is best, as cooking may diminish wine's nuances.

SAUSAGES & MEATBALLS

MAKING SAUSAGES WITHOUT A STUFFER

◆ ◆ ◆

It is entirely feasible to craft genuine homemade sausages without professional equipment. All you need is a pastry bag and sausage casings. With a bit of skill, the results can be exceptionally gratifying!

WORKSHOP: STUFFING A SAUSAGE

STEP 1

Soak the casings in warm water.

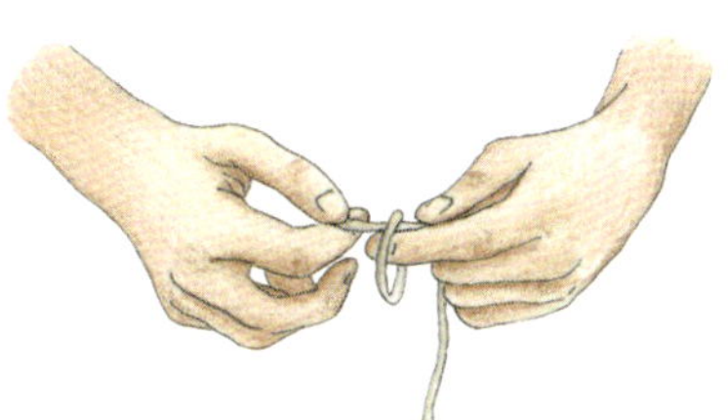

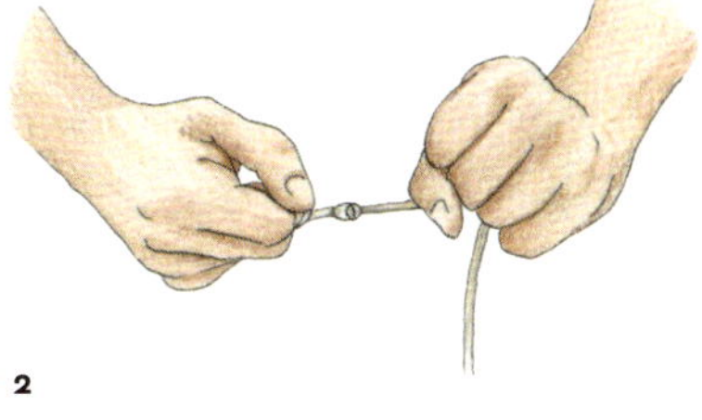

STEP 2

Tie a knot at one end of a casing.

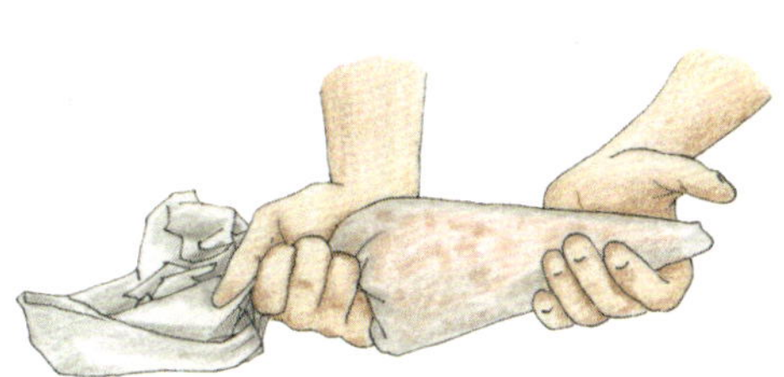

STEP 3

Fill a pastry bag with the sausage filling.

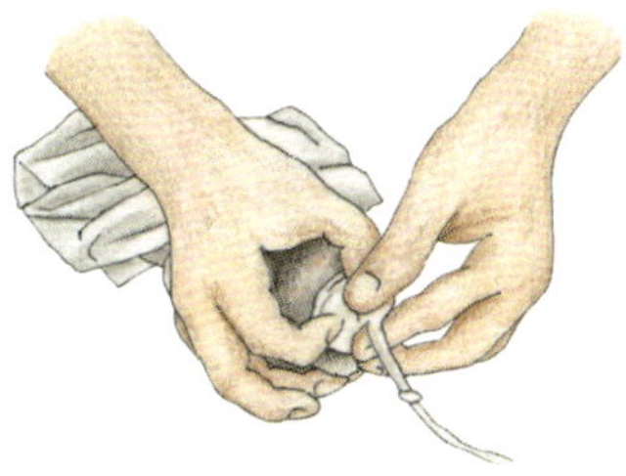

STEP 4

Slide the casing over the pastry bag.

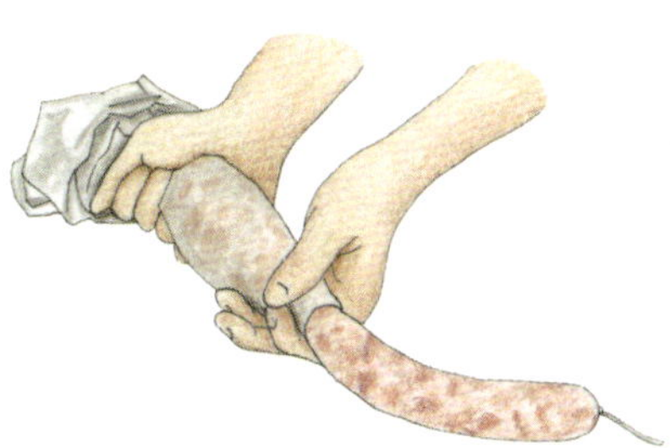

STEP 5

Squeeze all the meat into the casing, ensuring no air is trapped.

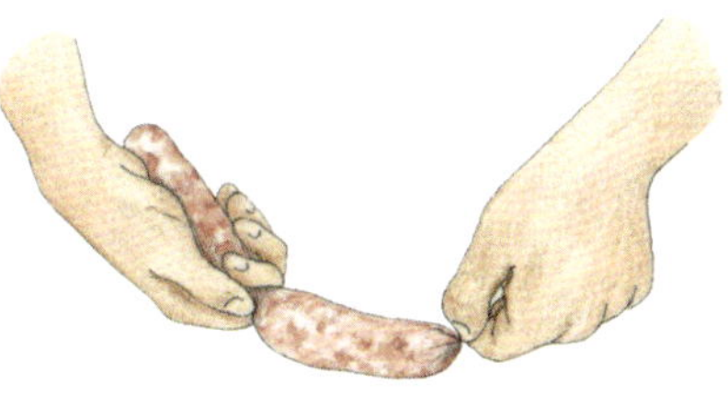

STEP 6

Portion sausages to the desired size by pinching one end and then twisting the sausage away from you to tighten.

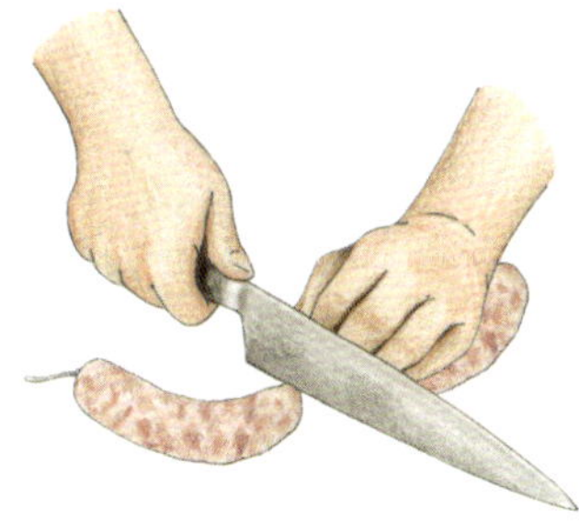

STEP 7

Once the sausages are portioned, snip off the ends.

FORMING MEATBALLS

◆ ◆ ◆

Any sausage recipe can be made into meatballs instead, skipping the stuffing and twisting. They're equally delicious!

WORKSHOP: FORMING MEATBALLS

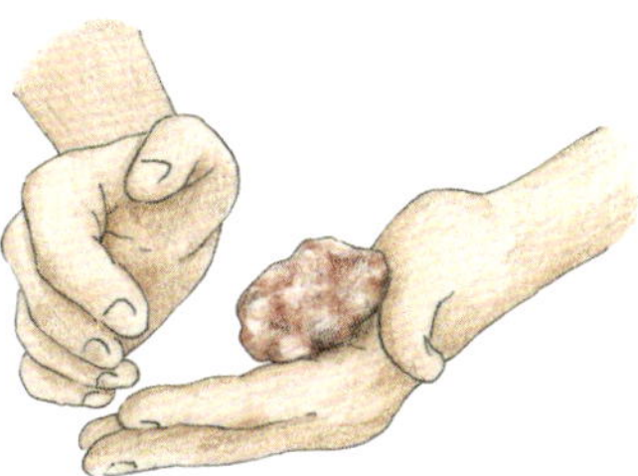

STEP 1

Pass a small ball of meat from one hand to the other, tossing it gently.

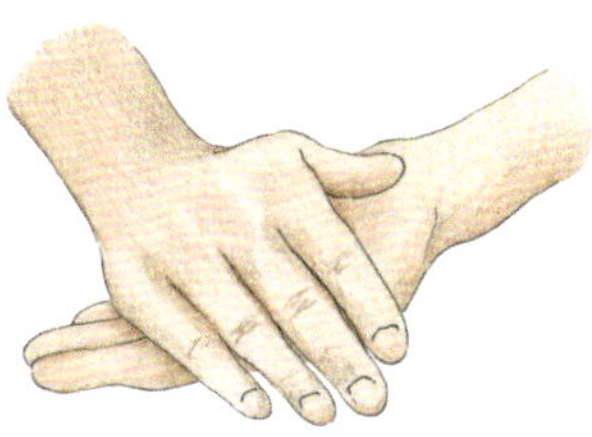

STEP 2

Compress the meat between the palms of your hands to release any trapped air.

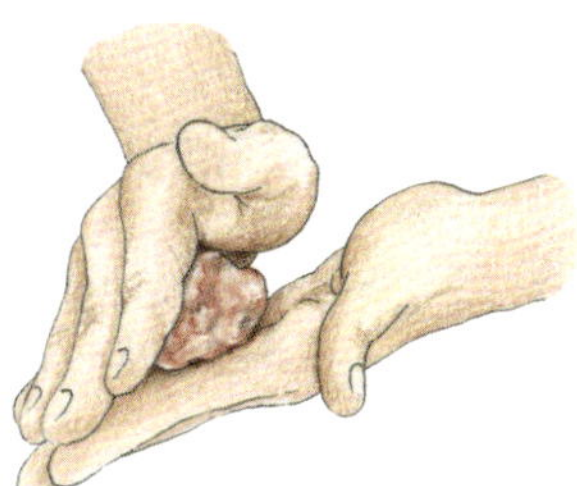

STEP 3

Roll the meatball between your hands until it forms a round shape.

MEATBALL SHAPES

ROUND MEATBALL

For more consistent cooking, it's best to bake meatballs in the oven.

FLATTENED MEATBALL

If you'd like to pan-fry, flatten the meatballs slightly and cook them similarly to a burger patty.

PREPARATION TIME
45 minutes

SAUSAGES & MEATBALLS

CHIPOLATAS

◆ ◆ ◆

INGREDIENTS

1 ⅛ pounds (600 g) whole pork belly or 1 pound (500 g) minced pork belly
1 pound (500 g) boneless pork shoulder or ground pork
3 teaspoons salt
4 pinches freshly ground pepper

MAKES 5 SERVINGS

Using a knife, remove the rind and any bones from the pork belly, making sure to keep the fat on the belly (see Workshop, p. 21). Chop the pork belly and pork shoulder into approximately ¼-inch (7 mm) pieces (see Workshop, p. 21).

Transfer the pork belly to a mixing bowl, add the salt and pepper, and mix by hand (see Workshop, p. 21) or in a mixer on low speed.

Add the pork shoulder.

Mix vigorously by hand or in a mixer on low speed for 5 minutes.

Shape into sausages (see Workshop, p. 135) or meatballs (see Workshop, p. 137).

Bake at 350°F (180°C) for 30 minutes or pan-fry until cooked through, and serve hot.

PREPARATION TIME
1 hour

SAUSAGES & MEATBALLS

HERB SAUSAGES AND MEATBALLS

◆◆◆

INGREDIENTS

1 ¼ pounds (650 g) whole pork belly or 1 pound (500 g) minced pork belly
1 pound (500 g) boneless pork shoulder or ground pork
4 garlic cloves
½ bunch parsley
½ bunch chervil
½ bunch tarragon
3 teaspoons salt
4 pinches freshly ground pepper

MAKES 5 SERVINGS

Using a knife, remove the rind and any bones from the pork belly, making sure to keep the fat on the belly (see Workshop, p. 21). Chop the pork belly and pork shoulder into approximately ¼-inch (7 mm) pieces (see Workshop, p. 21).

Peel the garlic, crush it with the palm of your hand or the blade of a knife, then mince finely. Roughly chop the parsley leaves, chervil, and tarragon.

In a mixing bowl, combine the minced pork belly with the salt and pepper. Mix by hand (see Workshop, p. 21) or in a mixer on a low speed.

Add the pork shoulder, garlic, and herbs and continue mixing until uniform.

Shape into sausages (see Workshop, p. 135) or meatballs (see Workshop, p. 137).

Bake at 350°F (180°C) for 30 minutes or pan-fry until cooked through, and serve hot.

PREPARATION TIME
50 minutes

SAUSAGES & MEATBALLS

CHEDDAR SAUSAGES

◆ ◆ ◆

INGREDIENTS

1 ⅛ pounds (600 g) whole pork belly or 1 pound (500 g) ground pork belly
1 pound (500 g) boneless pork shoulder or ground pork
5–6 ounces (150 g) cheddar cheese
3 teaspoons salt
4 pinches freshly ground pepper

MAKES 5 SERVINGS

Using a knife, remove the rind and any bones from the pork belly, making sure to keep the fat on the belly (see Workshop, p. 21). Cube the pork belly and pork shoulders into approximately ¼-inch (7 mm) pieces (see Workshop, p. 21).

Cut the cheddar into ½-inch (14 mm) cubes.

Place the pork belly in a mixing bowl, add the salt and pepper, and mix by hand (see Workshop, p. 21) or in a mixer on low speed.

If making sausages, add the pork shoulder and cheddar and continue mixing until uniform. If making meatballs, add the pork shoulder and mix until uniform, reserving the cheddar.

Stir vigorously by hand or in a mixer at low speed for 5 minutes.

Shape into sausages (see Workshop, p. 135) or meatballs (see Workshop, p. 137). If making meatballs, insert a cube or two of cheddar into the center of each ball, ensuring a melty cheddar core after cooking.

Bake at 350°F (180°C) for 30 minutes or pan-fry until cooked through, and serve hot.

PREPARATION TIME
45 minutes

SAUSAGES & MEATBALLS

MERGUEZ-STYLE MEATBALLS

◆ ◆ ◆

INGREDIENTS

10 ½ ounces (300 g) whole lamb belly or 9 ounces (250 g) ground lamb belly
1 ½ pounds (750 g) boneless lamb shoulder, whole or ground
1 teaspoon paprika
2 pinches ground cumin
2 pinches mild chili powder
3 teaspoons salt
4 pinches freshly ground pepper

MAKES 5 SERVINGS

Using a knife, remove the rind and any bones from the lamb belly, making sure to keep the fat on (see Workshop, p. 21). Chop the lamb belly and lamb shoulder into approximately ¼-inch (7 mm) pieces (see Workshop, p. 21).

Place the meat in a mixing bowl, add the paprika, cumin, chili powder, and salt and pepper, and mix by hand (see Workshop, p. 21) or on low speed with a mixer.

Shape into sausages (see Workshop, p. 135) or meatballs (see Workshop, p. 137).

Bake at 350°F (180°C) for 30 minutes or pan-fry until cooked through, and serve hot.

PREPARATION TIME
1 hour

SAUSAGES & MEATBALLS

BEAUJOLAIS SAUSAGES

◆ ◆ ◆

INGREDIENTS

½ yellow onion
2 shallots
1 tablespoon unsalted butter
¼ cup (50 g) chopped bacon
1 ⅛ pounds (600 g) whole pork belly or 1 pound (500 g) ground pork belly
1 pound (500 g) boneless pork shoulder or ground pork
3 teaspoons salt
4 pinches freshly ground pepper
¼ cup (60 g) Beaujolais (Gamay) wine

MAKES 5 SERVINGS

Coarsely chop the onion and shallots. In a medium skillet over medium heat, melt the butter and sauté the onion and shallots until they soften. Add the bacon for the last 30 seconds of cooking.

Using a knife, remove the rind and any bones from the pork belly, making sure to keep the fat on the belly (see Workshop, p. 21). Chop the pork belly and pork shoulder into approximately ¼-inch (7 mm) pieces (see Workshop, p. 21).

In a mixing bowl, combine the pork belly and the salt and pepper. Mix by hand (see Workshop, p. 21) or in a mixer on a low speed.

Add the pork shoulder, wine, shallots, onion, and bacon. Stir vigorously by hand or in a mixer on low mixer speed for 5 minutes.

Shape into sausages (see Workshop, p. 135) or meatballs (see Workshop, p. 137).

Bake at 350°F (180°C) for 30 minutes or pan-fry until cooked through, and serve hot.

PREPARATION TIME
45 minutes

SAUSAGES & MEATBALLS

MUSTARD MEATBALLS

◆ ◆ ◆

INGREDIENTS

1 ¼ pounds (650 g) whole pork belly or 1 pound (500 g) minced pork belly
1 pound (500 g) boneless pork shoulder or ground pork
3 teaspoons salt
4 pinches freshly ground pepper
½ cup (100 g) whole-grain mustard

MAKES 5 SERVINGS

Using a knife, remove the rind and any bones from the pork belly, making sure to keep the fat on the belly (see Workshop, p. 21). Chop the pork belly and pork shoulder into approximately ¼-inch (7 mm) pieces (see Workshop, p. 21).

Place the pork belly in a mixing bowl, add the salt and pepper, and mix by hand (see Workshop, p. 21) or in a mixer on low speed. Add the pork shoulder and mustard.

Vigorously mix by hand or in a mixer on low speed for 5 minutes.

Shape into meatballs (see Workshop, p. 137) or sausages (see Workshop, p. 135).

Bake at 350°F (180°C) for 30 minutes or pan-fry until cooked through, and serve hot.

PREPARATION TIME

1 hour 20 minutes

CABBAGE SAUSAGES

◆◆◆

INGREDIENTS

½ yellow onion
¾ pound (300 g) green cabbage
1 tablespoon unsalted butter
2 ounces (50 g) chopped bacon
1 ¼ pounds (650 g) whole pork belly or 14 ounces (400g) minced pork belly
14 ounces (400 g) boneless pork shoulder or ground pork (or other lean meat)
3 teaspoons salt
4 pinches freshly ground pepper

MAKES 5 SERVINGS

Roughly chop the onion. Slice the cabbage into thin strips.

In a medium skillet over medium heat, melt the butter and sauté the onion and cabbage until they soften. Add the bacon and continue to sauté for 1 minute, then drain the bacon on paper towels.

Using a knife, remove the rind and any bones from the pork belly, making sure to keep the fat on the belly (see Workshop, p. 21). Chop the pork belly and pork shoulder into approximately ¼-inch (7 mm) pieces (see Workshop, p. 21).

Place the pork belly and pork shoulder in a mixing bowl. Add the cabbage, onion, bacon, and salt and pepper.

Vigorously mix by hand (see Workshop, p. 21) or with a mixer on low speed for 5 minutes.

Shape into sausages (see Workshop, p. 135) or meatballs (see p. 137).

Bake at 350°F (180°C) for 30 minutes or pan-fry until cooked through, and serve hot.

PREPARATION TIME

1 hour 10 minutes minutes

SAUSAGES & MEATBALLS

THE MOUNTAINEER

◆ ◆ ◆

INGREDIENTS

1 pound (500 g) whole pork belly or ¾ pound (350 g) minced pork belly
1 pound (500 g) boneless pork shoulder or ground pork
5 ounces (150 g) chopped bacon
½ yellow onion
½ pound (200 g) Reblochon or Brie cheese
1 tablespoon unsalted butter
1 teaspoon salt
2 pinches freshly ground pepper
1 tablespoon white wine

MAKES 5 SERVINGS

Using a knife, remove the rind and any bones from the pork belly, making sure to keep the fat on the belly (see Workshop, p. 21). Chop the pork belly and pork shoulder into approximately ¼-inch (7 mm) pieces (see Workshop, p. 21).

Finely chop the onion. Cut the cheese into cubes twice the size of the pork belly dice.

In a medium skillet over medium heat, sauté the onion in butter until softened. Once softened, add bacon, cook 1 minute, then drain the bacon on paper towels.

Place the pork belly in a mixing bowl, add the salt and pepper, and then mix by hand (see Workshop, p. 21) or with a mixer on low speed. Add the pork shoulder, onion, bacon, wine, and if making sausages, the cheese. (If making meatballs, reserve the cheese for the shaping process.)

Vigorously mix by hand (see Workshop, p. 21) or in a mixer on low speed for 5 minutes.

Shape into sausages (see Workshop, p. 135) or meatballs (see Workshop, p. 137). If making meatballs, insert a cube or two of cheese into the center of each ball, ensuring a melty cheesy core after cooking.

Bake at 350°F (180°C) for 30 minutes or pan-fry until cooked through, and serve hot.

PREPARATION TIME
50 minutes

SAUSAGES & MEATBALLS

THAI MEATBALLS

◆ ◆ ◆

INGREDIENTS

¼ ounce (5 g) fresh lemongrass
1 ¼ ounces (5 g) fresh ginger
1 ¼ pounds (650 g) whole pork belly or 1 pound (500 g) minced pork belly
1 pound (500 g) boneless pork shoulder or ground pork (or other lean meat)
3 teaspoons salt
4 pinches freshly ground pepper
½ ounce (2 g) ground turmeric
1 teaspoon soy sauce

MAKES 5 SERVINGS

Finely chop the lemongrass and grate the ginger.

Using a knife, remove the rind and any bones from the pork belly, making sure to keep the fat on the belly (see Workshop, p. 21). Chop the pork belly and pork shoulder into approximately ¼-inch (7 mm) pieces (see Workshop, p. 21).

Place the pork belly in a mixing bowl, add the salt and pepper, then mix by hand (see Workshop, p. 21) or in a mixer on low speed. Add the pork shoulder, lemongrass, ginger, turmeric, and soy sauce.

Mix vigorously by hand or with the mixer on low speed for 5 minutes. Shape into sausages (see Workshop, p. 135) or meatballs (see Workshop, p. 137).

Bake at 350°F (180°C) for 30 minutes or pan-fry until cooked through, and serve hot.

PREPARATION TIME

1 hour 15 minutes

SAUSAGES & MEATBALLS

COUNTRYSIDE MEATBALLS

◆ ◆ ◆

INGREDIENTS

½ pound (250 g) russet potatoes
1 pound (500 g) whole pork belly or ¾ pound (350 g) minced pork belly
¾ pound (350 g) boneless pork shoulder or ground pork
1 shallot
2 garlic cloves
3 sprigs parsley
3 teaspoons salt
4 pinches freshly ground pepper

MAKES 5 SERVINGS

Boil the potatoes until tender. Drain and set aside to cool.

Using a knife, remove the rind and any bones from the pork belly, making sure to keep the fat on the belly (see Workshop, p. 21). Chop the pork belly and pork shoulder into approximately ¼-inch (7 mm) pieces (see Workshop, p. 21).

Cut the boiled potatoes into ½-inch (7-mm) cubes. Finely chop the shallot, garlic, and parsley leaves.

Place the pork belly in a mixing bowl, add the salt and pepper, then mix by hand (see Workshop, p. 21) or in a mixer on low speed. Add the pork shoulder, potatoes, shallot, garlic, and parsley.

Mix vigorously by hand or in a mixer on low speed for 5 minutes. Shape into meatballs (see Workshop, p. 137) or sausages (see Workshop, p. 135).

Bake at 350°F (180°C) for 30 minutes or pan-fry until cooked through, and serve hot.

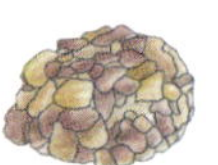

PÂTÉS EN CROÛTE

PREPARING SHORTCRUST PASTRY

◆ ◆ ◆

To make a pâté en croûte, one must make (or buy) a shortcrust pastry, master the molding of the pastry, and ensure the pie is well sealed around the filling. These essential techniques guarantee a splendid result!

WORKSHOP: SHORTCRUST PASTRY

4 cups (500 g) all-purpose flour | 1 cup (2 sticks or 250 g) unsalted butter, chilled | 1 teaspoon salt
½ cup (115 g) ice water | 7 egg yolks

STEP 1

Dice the cold butter.

STEP 2

Pour flour onto a work surface and mix in the salt.

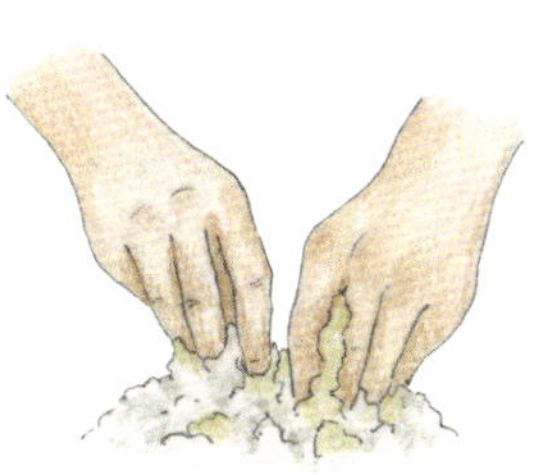

STEP 3

Blend in the butter cubes with your fingertips until a sandy texture forms.

STEP 4

Make a well in the center and gradually incorporate the water and egg yolks, mixing to combine.

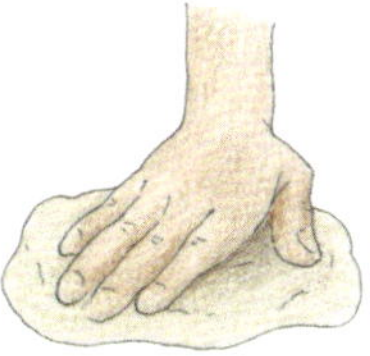

STEP 5

Knead the dough using your palm, until a homogenous dough forms. Shape the dough into a rectangle, then wrap in plastic wrap and refrigerate for at least 1 hour and up to 2 days.

ASSEMBLING THE PASTRY SHELL

◆ ◆ ◆

Crafting a pâté en croûte is a technical art that combines the finesse of both charcuterie and patisserie. Proper assembly of the pastry pieces is essential to the stability of the finished dish, ensuring there is no leakage of the flavorful juices.

WORKSHOP: PASTRY SHELL ASSEMBLY

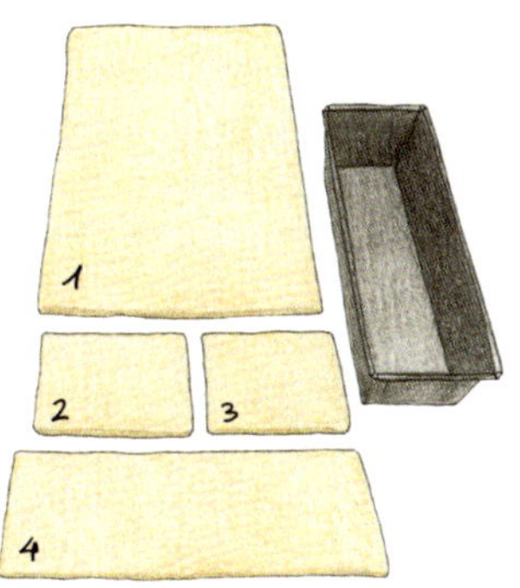

STEP 1

Roll the dough out to a ⅛-inch (3-mm) thickness.
1. Main piece of dough
2 and 3. Dough for sides.
4. Dough for cover.

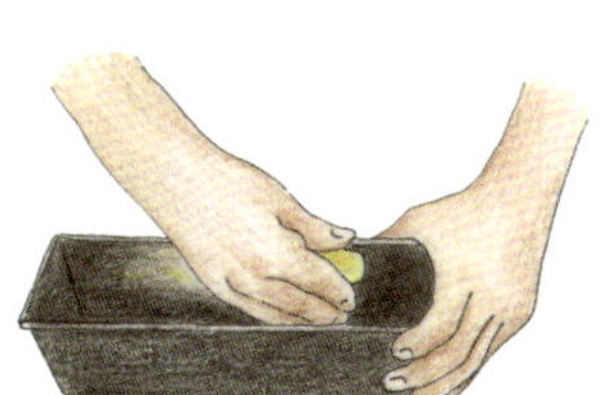

STEP 2

Butter the mold.

STEP 3

Lower the main piece of dough into the bottom of the mold.

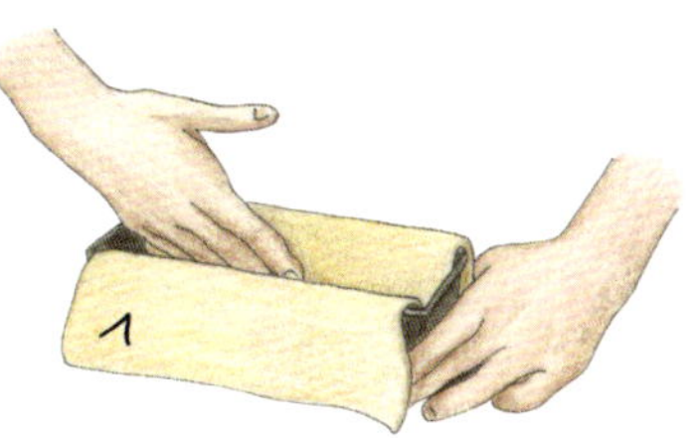

STEP 4

Firmly press the dough against the mold's edges.

STEP 5

Gently press down on the dough so it adheres to the bottom of the mold.

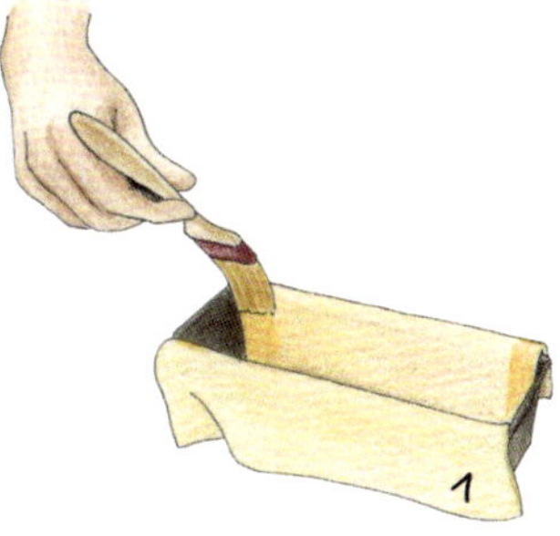

STEP 6

Brush the edges of the main dough lightly with beaten egg.

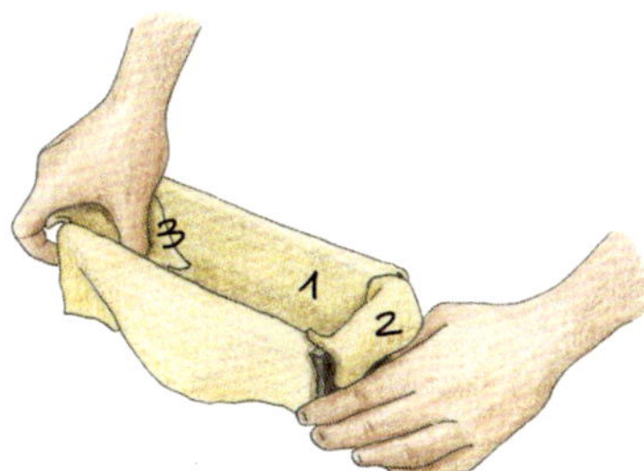

STEP 7

Add the side pieces of dough into the mold and press gently onto the sides.

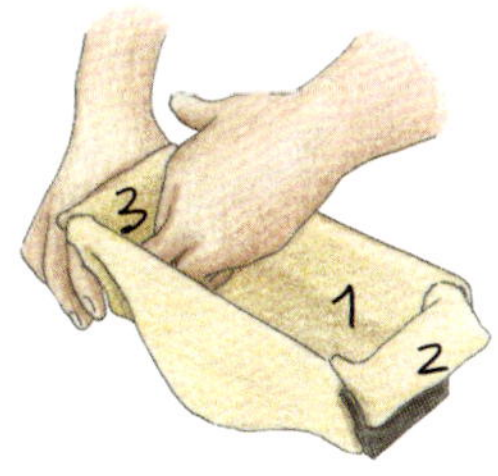

STEP 8

Seal the side pieces of the dough to the main dough, pressing gently with your fingertips.

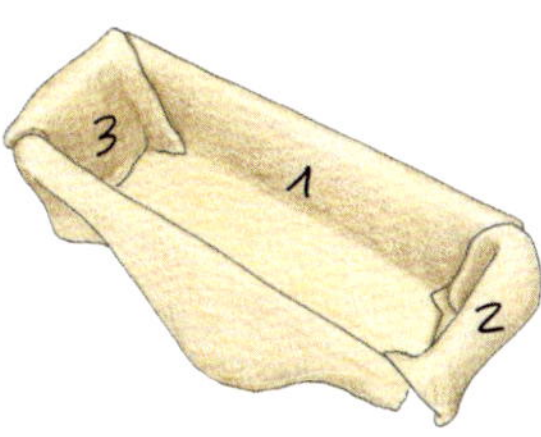

STEP 9

The mold is ready to be filled.

SEALING A PÂTÉ EN CROÛTE

◆ ◆ ◆

Sealing the pâté en croûte requires precision. A meticulous closure ensures the pie's juices remain intact after baking. Master this technique by following the detailed steps on the following page.

WORKSHOP: SEALING STEP BY STEP

STEP 1

Firmly pack the filling into the crust-lined mold.

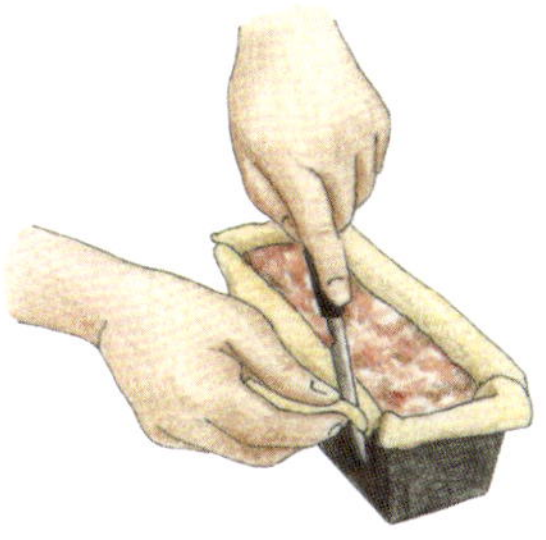

STEP 2

Trim any excess dough, leaving about ¾ inch (2 cm) of overhang.

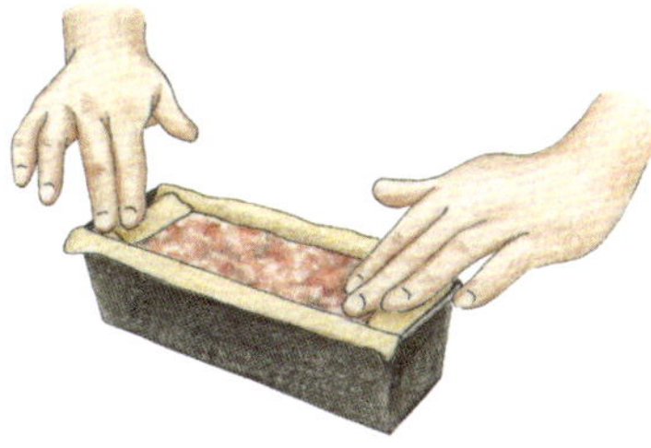

STEP 3

Fold the overhanging dough over the short sides.

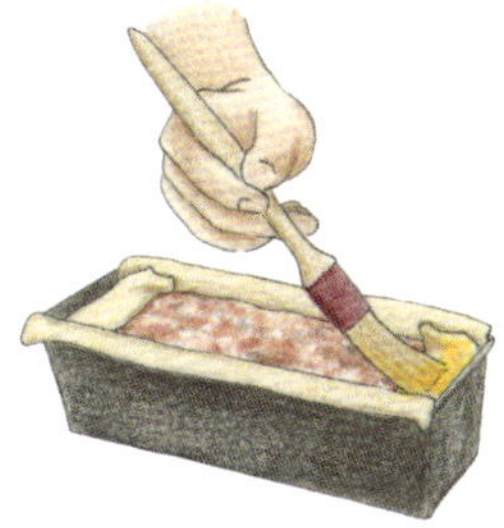

STEP 4

Brush the short sides with a light coat of beaten egg.

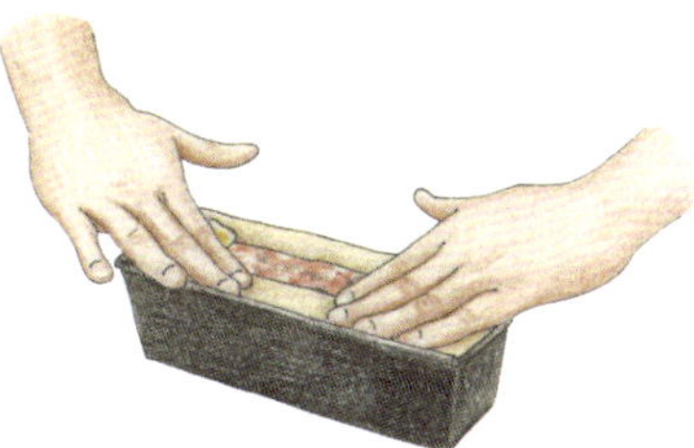

STEP 5

Fold the overhanging dough over the long sides.

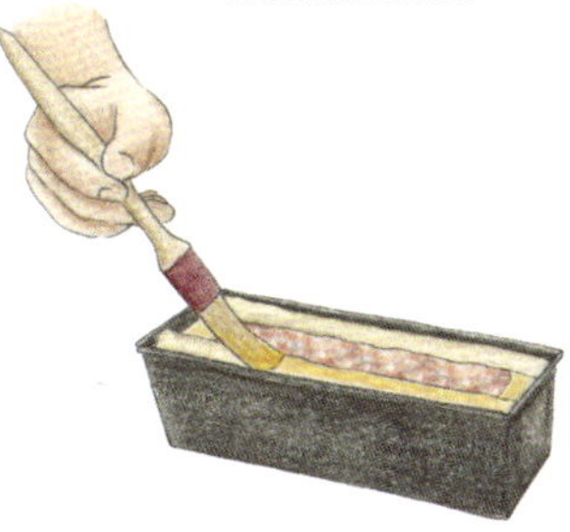

STEP 6

Brush the long sides with a light coat of beaten egg.

STEP 7

Place the dough for the cover on top.

STEP 8

Press down with your hands along the edges to seal the doughs together.

STEP 9

Brush with beaten egg.

STEP 10

Carefully decorate the top using a knife's blunt edge.

STEP 11

Cut one or two vents into the dough using the tip of the knife.

STEP 12

The pâté en croûte is now oven-ready.

PREPARATION TIME
1 hour 45 minutes

COOKING TIME
1 hour 10 minutes

RESTING TIME
Overnight

PÂTÉS EN CROÛTE

CHICKEN & CHILE PÂTÉ EN CROÛTE

◆ ◆ ◆

INGREDIENTS

1 pound (500 g) whole pork belly or 1 pound (500 g) ground pork belly
1 pound (500 g) boneless skinless chicken breast
1 small fresh Espelette pepper
2 pinches ground Espelette pepper
3 teaspoons salt
2 pinches freshly ground pepper
3 large eggs, divided
3 ½ tablespoons heavy cream
1 pound (500 g) shortcrust pastry (recipe p. 161)
1 ½ tablespoons unsalted butter, for greasing the mold
2 ⅓ cups (550 g) aspic, at room temperature (recipe p. 171)

MAKES 6 SERVINGS

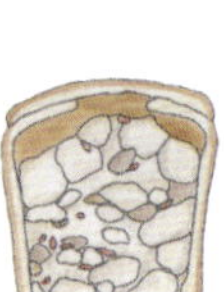

Using a knife, if necessary, debone the veal breast and Chop into approximately ¼-inch (7 mm) pieces (see Workshop, p. 21). Cut the chicken into ½-inch (1 ½-cm) cubes (see Workshop, p. 51).

Transfer the veal to a mixing bowl, add the salt and pepper, and mix by hand (see Workshop, p. 21) or with a mixer on low speed.

Add 1 egg and the cream and mix until uniform. Add the chicken. Vigorously mix by hand or in a mixer on low speed for 5 minutes. Refrigerate.

Grease the mold with the butter. Beat the remaining 2 eggs. Roll the dough to ⅛-inch (3-mm) thickness, cut it, and line the mold (see Workshop, p. 163). Add the filling. Seal the crust with the top piece of dough (see Workshop, p. 165). Cut 1 or 2 round holes in the top.

Place the mold in a cold oven. Set the temperature to 350°F (180°C) and bake using the convection setting (if possible) for 1 hour 10 minutes. Alternatively, monitor with a cooking thermometer and remove when the internal temperature reaches 145°F (64°C).

Allow it to rest for 30 minutes at room temperature, then refrigerate overnight. The next day, pour in the aspic as directed on p. 171. Chill for at least 1 hour before serving.

PREPARATION TIME
2 hours

COOKING TIME
1 hour 10 minutes

RESTING TIME
Overnight

PÂTÉS EN CROÛTE

DUCK & FIG PÂTÉ EN CROÛTE

◆ ◆ ◆

INGREDIENTS

1 pound (500 g) whole pork belly or 14 ounces (400 g) ground pork belly
1 pound (500 g) duck breast
⅓ pound (150 g) boneless skinless chicken breast
3 ½ ounces (100 g) dried figs
2 teaspoons salt
3 pinches freshly ground pepper
3 large eggs, divided
2 cups (500 g) heavy cream
1 ½ tablespoons unsalted butter, for greasing the mold
1 pound (500 g) shortcrust pastry (recipe p. 161)
1 teaspoon alcohol of your choice
2 ⅓ cups (550 g) aspic, at room temperature (recipe p. 171)

MAKES 6 SERVINGS

Using a knife, remove the rind and any bones from the pork belly, making sure to keep the fat on the belly (see Workshop, p. 21). Chop the pork belly into approximately ¼-inch (7 mm) pieces (see Workshop, p. 21).

Remove the skin from the duck breast and cut into ½-inch (1 ½-cm) cubes. Cube the chicken into ½-inch (1 ½-cm) cubes, and chill. Cut the figs into ¼-inch (¾-cm) pieces.

Place the pork belly in a mixing bowl, add the salt and pepper, and mix by hand (see Workshop, p. 21) or in a mixer on a low speed. Pour 1 egg and the cream into the bowl and blend until the mixture becomes uniform. Add the duck and figs, mixing vigorously. Add the chicken cubes and stir until evenly distributed in the filling. Place in the refrigerator to chill.

Grease the mold with the butter. Beat the remaining 2 eggs. Roll the dough to ⅛-inch (3-mm) thickness, cut it, and line the mold (see Workshop, p. 163). Add the filling. Seal the crust with the top piece of dough (see Workshop, p. 165). Cut 1 or 2 round holes in the top.

Place the mold in a cold oven. Set the temperature to 350°F (180°C) and bake using the convection setting (if possible) for 1 hour 10 minutes. Alternatively, monitor with a cooking thermometer and remove when the internal temperature reaches 145°F (64°C).

Allow it to rest for 30 minutes at room temperature, then refrigerate overnight. The next day, pour in the aspic (see Workshop, p. 171). Chill for at least 1 hour before serving.

ASPIC

THE ESSENTIALS

◆◆◆

Aspic (savory meat jelly) is frequently incorporated into charcuterie recipes. The way it's used depends on the recipe. For instance, in a pâté en croute, aspic is primarily used to seal the space between the crust and the filling after cooking, while it provides structure to pressed dishes.

WORKSHOP: ASPIC

Aspic is a preparation made by combining a gelling agent with a liquid, usually a meat broth. Gelling agents can derive from animals (pigs' or calves' trotters are often used), or plants (pectin, a plant carbohydrate, or agar-agar, made from seaweed).

Both animal- and plant-based gelatin are viable options for aspic, but animal gelatin is more commonly used as it ensures a better hold for the preparation. Plant-based gelatin is preferred for vegetarian dishes, such as vegetable terrines.

Pâté en croûte

Pressed dish

QUICK AND SIMPLE ASPIC

Soak 50 grams (about 3 sheets or 1 ½ teaspoons powdered) gelatin in cold water until the sheets have softened or the powder has dissolved. In the meantime, bring 2 ⅛ cups (500 g) of meat broth to a boil in a saucepan, then remove from heat. Remove the gelatin sheets from the water, squeezing out any extra moisture. Add the gelatin to the hot meat broth, stirring to dissolve. Cool to room temperature before using (or refrigerate for up to 2 days and then rewarm and let cool to room temperature).

For a pâté en croûte, pour the aspic through openings made in the top of the dough, ensuring it doesn't overflow. Incorporated into a pressed dish, the aspic ensures perfect slice integrity and a unique aromatic profile, thanks to its pairing with the cooking broth.

PREPARATION TIME
2 hours

COOKING TIME
1 hour 10 minutes

RESTING TIME
Overnight

GREEN PEPPERCORN PÂTÉ EN CROÛTE

◆◆◆

INGREDIENTS

1 pound (500 grams) whole pork belly or 1 pound (500 grams) minced pork belly
1 pound (500 grams) pork tenderloin
3 teaspoons salt
½ teaspoon freshly ground pepper
3 large eggs, divided
3 ½ tablespoons heavy cream
1 ½ teaspoons whole green peppercorns
1 ½ tablespoons unsalted butter, for greasing the mold
1 pound (500 grams) shortcrust pastry (recipe p. 161)
2 ⅓ cups (550 g) aspic, at room temperature (recipe p. 171)

MAKES 6 SERVINGS

Using a knife, remove the rind and any bones from the pork belly, making sure to keep the fat on the belly (see Workshop, p. 21). Chop the pork belly into approximately ¼-inch (7 mm) pieces (see Workshop, p. 21).

Cut the pork tenderloin into ½-inch (1 ¼-cm) cubes (see Workshop, p. 51).

Place the pork belly in a mixing bowl, add the salt and pepper, then mix by hand or in a mixer on low speed.

Pour 1 egg and the cream into the bowl and blend until the mixture becomes uniform. Add the pork tenderloin and whole green peppercorns. Mix vigorously by hand or in a mixer on low speed for 5 minutes. Refrigerate.

Grease the mold with the butter. Beat the remaining 2 eggs. Roll the dough to ⅛-inch (3-mm) thickness, cut it, and line the mold (see Workshop, p. 163). Add the filling. Seal the crust with the top piece of dough (see Workshop, p. 165). Cut 1 or 2 round holes in the top.

Place the mold in a cold oven. Set the temperature to 350°F (180°C) and bake using the convection setting (if possible) for 1 hour 10 minutes. Alternatively, monitor with a cooking thermometer and remove when the internal temperature reaches 145°F (64°C).

Allow it to rest for 30 minutes at room temperature, then refrigerate overnight. The next day, pour in the aspic as directed on p. 171. Chill for at least 1 hour before serving.

PREPARATION TIME
2 hours

COOKING TIME
1 hour 10 minutes

RESTING TIME
Overnight

PÂTÉS EN CROÛTE

CHICKEN & PISTACHIOS PÂTÉ EN CROÛTE

◆ ◆ ◆

INGREDIENTS

1 pound (500 g) whole pork belly or 1 pound (500 g) ground pork belly
1 pound (500 g) boneless skinless chicken breast
3 teaspoons salt
3 pinches freshly ground pepper
3 large eggs, divided
¼ cup (50 ml/50 g) heavy cream
½ cup (100 g) shelled, unsalted pistachios
1 ½ tablespoons unsalted butter, for greasing the mold
1 pound (500 g) shortcrust pastry (recipe p. 161)
2 ⅓ cups (550 g) aspic, at room temperature (recipe p. 171)

MAKES 6 SERVINGS

Using a knife, remove the rind and any bones from the pork belly, making sure to keep the fat on the belly (see Workshop, p. 21). Chop the pork belly into approximately ¼-inch (7 mm) pieces (see Workshop, p. 21).

Cut the chicken into ½-inch (1 ½-cm) cubes (see Workshop, p. 51).

Place the pork belly in a mixing bowl, add the salt and pepper, and mix by hand (see Workshop, p. 21) or in a mixer at low speed.

Add 1 egg and the cream to the bowl and blend until the mixture becomes uniform. Add the chicken and pistachios, then mix vigorously by hand or with a mixer on low speed for 5 minutes. Refrigerate.

Grease the mold with the butter. Beat the remaining 2 eggs. Roll the dough to ⅛-inch (3-mm) thickness, cut it, and line the mold (see Workshop, p. 163). Add the filling. Seal the crust with the top piece of dough (see Workshop, p. 165). Cut 1 or 2 round holes in the top.

Place the mold in a cold oven. Set the temperature to 350°F (180°C) and bake using the convection setting (if possible) for 1 hour 10 minutes. Alternatively, monitor with a cooking thermometer and remove when the internal temperature reaches 145°F (64°C).

Allow it to rest for 30 minutes at room temperature, then refrigerate overnight. The next day, pour in the aspic as directed on p. 171. Chill for at least 1 hour before serving.

PREPARATION TIME
2 hours 15 minutes

COOKING TIME
1 hour 10 minutes

RESTING TIME
Overnight

CHICKEN & APPLE PÂTÉ EN CROÛTE

◆ ◆ ◆

INGREDIENTS

1 pound (500 g) whole pork belly or 1 pound (500 g) ground pork belly
1 pound (500 g) boneless skinless chicken breast
1 tablespoon unsalted butter, plus 1 ½ tablespoons for greasing the mold
1 apple
1 tablespoon granulated sugar
½ teaspoon freshly ground pepper
3 large eggs, divided
¼ cup (60 g) heavy cream
1 pound (500 g) shortcrust pastry (recipe p. 161)
2 ⅓ cups (550 g) aspic, at room temperature (recipe p. 171)

MAKES 6 SERVINGS

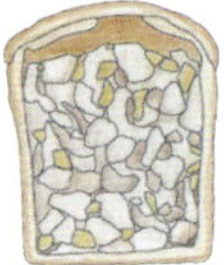

Using a knife, remove the rind and any bones from the pork belly, making sure to keep the fat on the belly (see Workshop, p. 21). Chop the pork belly into approximately ¼-inch (7 mm) pieces (see Workshop, p. 21).

Cut the chicken into ½-inch (1 ½-cm) cubes (see Workshop, p. 51).

Peel, core, and quarter the apple. Dice it into ¼-inch (7 mm) pieces.

In a small skillet over medium heat, melt 1 tablespoon of the butter, and sauté the apple for 2 minutes. Sprinkle with the sugar and sauté for another 30 seconds, stirring continuously.

Place the ground pork belly in a mixing bowl, add the salt and pepper, and mix by hand (see Workshop, p. 21) or in a mixer at low speed.

Add 1 egg and the cream to the bowl and blend until the mixture becomes uniform. Incorporate the chicken and apples, then mix vigorously by hand or with a mixer on low speed for 5 minutes. Refrigerate.

Grease the mold with the butter. Beat the remaining 2 eggs. Roll the dough to ⅛-inch (3-mm) thickness, cut it, and line the mold (see Workshop, p. 163). Add the filling. Seal the crust with the top piece of dough (see Workshop, p. 165). Cut 1 or 2 round holes in the top.

Place the mold in a cold oven. Set the temperature to 350°F (180°C) and bake using the convection setting (if possible) for 1 hour 10 minutes. Alternatively, monitor with a cooking thermometer and remove when the internal temperature reaches 145°F (64°C).

Allow it to rest for 30 minutes at room temperature, then refrigerate overnight. The next day, pour in the aspic as directed on p. 171. Chill for at least 1 hour before serving.

PREPARATION TIME
1 hour

COOKING TIME
1 hour 10 minutes

RESTING TIME
Overnight

RUSTIC PÂTÉ EN CROÛTE

◆ ◆ ◆

INGREDIENTS

14 ounces (400 g) whole pork belly or 10 ounces (300 g) minced pork belly
6 sprigs parsley
2 shallots
10 ounces (300 g) boneless pork shoulder
2 ounces (50 g) bread, cubed
½ cup (100 g) heavy cream
3 teaspoons salt
3 pinches freshly ground pepper
7 ounces (200 g) chicken livers
4 large eggs, divided
1 pound (500 g) shortcrust pastry (recipe p. 161)
1 ½ tablespoons unsalted butter, for greasing the mold
2 ⅓ cups (550 g) aspic, at room temperature (recipe p. 171)

MAKES 6 SERVINGS

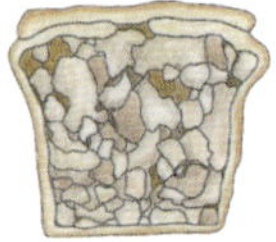

Using a knife, remove the rind and any bones from the pork belly, making sure to keep the fat on the belly (see Workshop, p. 21). Chop the pork belly into approximately ¼-inch (7 mm) pieces (see Workshop, p. 21).

Finely chop the parsley leaves and shallots. Cut the pork shoulder into approximately ½-inch (1 ½-cm) cubes (see Workshop, p. 51).

Place the bread in a medium saucepan, add the cream, and simmer over medium heat for 2 minutes. Add the parsley and shallot, and simmer for an additional 2 minutes.

Place the pork belly in a mixing bowl, add the salt and pepper, and mix either by hand (see Workshop, p. 21) or with a mixer on low speed. Add 2 eggs and continue mixing until the mixture is uniform.

Add the chicken livers, pork shoulder, and the cream-bread-parsley-shallot mixture. Mix vigorously by hand or with a mixer on low speed for 5 minutes, then refrigerate.

Grease the mold with the butter. Beat the remaining 2 eggs. Roll the dough to ⅛-inch (3-mm) thickness, cut it, and line the mold (see Workshop, p. 163). Add the filling. Seal the crust with the top piece of dough (see Workshop, p. 165). Cut 1 or 2 round holes in the top.

Place the mold in a cold oven. Set the temperature to 350°F (180°C) and bake using the convection setting (if possible) for 1 hour 10 minutes. Alternatively, monitor with a cooking thermometer and remove when the internal temperature reaches 145°F (64°C).

Allow it to rest for 30 minutes at room temperature, then refrigerate overnight. The next day, pour in the aspic as directed on p. 171. Chill for at least 1 hour before serving.

PREPARATION TIME
1 hour

COOKING TIME
1 hour 10 minutes

RESTING TIME
Overnight

PÂTÉS EN CROÛTE

MOREL MUSHROOM PÂTÉ EN CROÛTE

◆ ◆ ◆

INGREDIENTS

1 ounce (30 g) dried morels
2 cups (470 g) water
1 pound (500 g) whole pork belly or 14 ounces (400 g) minced pork belly
14 ounces (400 g) boneless pork shoulder
½ cup (100 g) heavy cream
3 teaspoons salt
3 pinches freshly ground pepper
3 large eggs, divided
1 pound (500 g) shortcrust pastry (recipe p. 161)
1 ½ tablespoons unsalted butter, for greasing the mold
2 ⅓ cups (550 g) aspic, at room temperature (recipe p. 171)

MAKES 6 SERVINGS

Soak the morels in the water. Once softened, change the water and soak for another 5 minutes. Repeat this process three times to thoroughly remove any dirt. Drain well.

While the morels soak, using a knife, remove the rind and any bones from the pork belly, making sure to keep the fat on the belly (see Workshop, p. 21). Chop the pork belly into approximately ¼-inch (7 mm) pieces (see Workshop, p. 21). Cut the pork shoulder into ½-inch (1 ½-cm) cubes (see Workshop, p. 51).

In a small saucepan over medium heat, warm the cream. Reduce heat to low, stir in the morels, and cook for 5 minutes. Remove the morels, let them cool, and then cut them into quarters. Discard the cream.

Place the pork belly in a mixing bowl, add the salt and pepper, and mix either by hand (see Workshop, p. 21) or with a mixer on low speed. Add 1 egg and mix until uniform. Add the pork shoulder and morels. Mix vigorously by hand or with a mixer on low speed for 5 minutes. Refrigerate.

Grease the mold with the butter. Beat the remaining 2 eggs. Roll the dough to ⅛-inch (3-mm) thickness, cut it, and line the mold (see Workshop, p. 163). Add the filling. Seal the crust with the top piece of dough (see Workshop, p. 165). Cut 1 or 2 round holes in the top.

Place the mold in a cold oven. Set the temperature to 350°F (180°C) and bake using the convection setting (if possible) for 1 hour 10 minutes. Alternatively, monitor with a cooking thermometer and remove when the internal temperature reaches 145°F (64°C).

Allow it to rest for 30 minutes at room temperature, then refrigerate overnight. The next day, pour in the aspic as directed on p. 171. Chill for at least 1 hour before serving.

MUSHROOMS

FRAGRANCE OF THE FOREST FLOOR

◆ ◆ ◆

We often hear the term "forest terrine." Yet this general name doesn't specify which type or types of mushrooms are used. The possibilities are vast. Mushrooms can be the star of a dish, or that extra touch that makes all the difference!

WORKSHOP:
TIPS FOR PAIRING MUSHROOMS AND CHARCUTERIE

WHITE BUTTON MUSHROOM

Agaricus bisporus

While the white button mushroom may not have the prestige of some of its relatives, it plays a key role in the elite world of pâtés and terrines. Here, it's essential for preparing a "gratin": sautéing shallots and mushrooms over medium heat, then adding parsley and chicken livers at the end to give them color. This "gratin" is then minced and mixed with meat, elevating both pâtés and terrines.

MOREL

Morchella esculenta

Morels hold a top-tier spot in charcuterie. A notable perk is that they're one of the few mushrooms available out of season, given their long shelf life when dried. Their texture and taste shine when roughly chopped in meat pies and terrines. Morels cooked in cream perfectly complement a puff pastry shell.

BLACK TRUFFLE

Tuber melanosporum

Undoubtedly the most esteemed of mushrooms, black truffles enhance almost all charcuterie preparations, from pâtés to terrines. While sometimes diluted with aromas and oils, they're best enjoyed fresh between January and February. Add them as chunks or slices to bring a note of freshness to dishes.

PORCINI MUSHROOM

Boletus edulis

Known for its distinctive hazelnut flavor, the porcini mushroom (or bolete) is highly prized and easy to integrate, in chunks, into a terrine. The Bordeaux variety is particularly renowned.

HORN OF PLENTY

Craterellus cornucopioides

These mushrooms, also called "trumpets of the dead" because they are ready to harvest around All Souls Day, are ideal for flavoring a terrine or pâté en croûte. They have thin, fragrantly scented flesh with a faintly bitter taste, and their deep black color offers visually appealing contrast.

PREPARATION TIME
2 hours

COOKING TIME
1 hour 10 minutes

RESTING TIME
Overnight

PÂTÉS EN CROÛTE

COULIBIAC-STYLE PÂTÉ EN CROÛTE

◆ ◆ ◆

INGREDIENTS

½ cup (100 g) semolina
4 cups (about 1 kg) water
5 large eggs, divided
1 tablespoon unsalted butter, plus 1 ½ tablespoons for greasing the mold
3 ½ ounces (15 g) spinach (about 3 ½ cups)
4 pinches salt
4 pinches freshly ground pepper
½ bunch parsley
1 bunch tarragon
1 ⅓ pounds (600 g) salmon fillet
1 pound (500 g) shortcrust pastry (recipe p. 161)
2 ⅓ cups (550 g) aspic, at room temperature (recipe p. 171)

MAKES 6 SERVINGS

Place the semolina in a medium heatproof bowl. In a medium saucepan, bring the water to a boil. Scoop out ½ cup (115 g) and pour it over the semolina. Set aside. Add 3 eggs to the saucepan, reduce the heat, and hard boil them for 10 minutes in simmering water. While the eggs boil, prepare a bowl of ice water. Transfer the boiled eggs to the ice water to cool.

In a medium skillet over medium heat, melt 1 tablespoon of the butter and cook the spinach for 1 minute. Season with 1 pinch each of the salt and pepper.

Finely chop the parsley leaves and tarragon. Peel and coarsely chop the boiled eggs and mix with the spinach. Season with 1 pinch each of the salt and pepper. Fluff the semolina using a fork. Mix in the parsley and tarragon.

Skin the salmon and slice it into two pieces, each the length of the mold. Season each piece with 1 pinch each of the salt and pepper.

Grease the mold with the butter. Beat the remaining 2 eggs. Roll the dough to ⅛-inch (3-mm) thickness, cut it, and line the mold (see Workshop, p. 163). Evenly layer the bottom with half of the semolina mixture. Next, add half of the salmon. Top with all of the spinach and egg mixture. Add the remaining salmon. Finish with another layer of the semolina mixture. Seal the crust with the top piece of dough (see Workshop, p. 165). Cut 1 or 2 round holes in the top.

Place the mold in a cold oven. Set the temperature to 350°F (180°C) and bake using the convection setting (if possible) for 1 hour 10 minutes. Alternatively, monitor with a cooking thermometer and remove when the internal temperature reaches 145°F (64°C). Allow it to rest for 30 minutes at room temperature, then refrigerate overnight. The next day, pour in the aspic as directed on p. 171. Chill for at least 1 hour before serving.

PREPARATION TIME
2 hours 20 minutes

COOKING TIME
1 hour 10 minutes

RESTING TIME
Overnight

PÂTÉS EN CROÛTE

PORK-FREE PÂTÉ EN CROÛTE

◆ ◆ ◆

INGREDIENTS

1 pound (500 g) whole veal breast or 1 pound (500 g) ground veal
1 pound (500 g) boneless skinless chicken breast
2 teaspoons salt
3 pinches freshly ground pepper
3 large eggs, divided
3 ¼ tablespoons heavy cream
1 ½ tablespoons unsalted butter, for greasing the mold
1 pound (500 g) shortcrust pastry (recipe p. 161)
2 ⅓ cups (550 g) aspic, at room temperature (recipe p. 171)

MAKES 6 SERVINGS

Using a knife, if necessary, debone the veal breast and chop it into approximately ¼-inch (7 mm) pieces (see Workshop, p. 21). Cut the chicken into ½-inch (1 ½-cm) cubes (see Workshop, p. 51).

Transfer the veal to a mixing bowl, add the salt and pepper, and mix by hand (see Workshop, p. 21) or with a mixer on low speed.

Add 1 egg and the cream and mix until uniform. Add the chicken. Vigorously mix by hand or in a mixer on low speed for 5 minutes. Refrigerate.

Grease the mold with the butter. Beat the remaining 2 eggs. Roll the dough to ⅛-inch (3-mm) thickness, cut it, and line the mold (see Workshop, p. 163). Add the filling. Seal the crust with the top piece of dough (see Workshop, p. 165). Cut 1 or 2 round holes in the top.

Place the mold in a cold oven. Set the temperature to 350°F (180°C) and bake using the convection setting (if possible) for 1 hour 10 minutes. Alternatively, monitor with a cooking thermometer and remove when the internal temperature reaches 145°F (64°C).

Allow it to rest for 30 minutes at room temperature, then refrigerate overnight. The next day, pour in the aspic as directed on p. 171. Chill for at least 1 hour before serving.

PREPARATION TIME
2 hours

COOKING TIME
1 hour 10 minutes

RESTING TIME
Overnight

DUCK & OLIVES PÂTÉ EN CROÛTE

◆ ◆ ◆

INGREDIENTS

1 pound (500 g) whole pork belly or 1 pound (500 g) ground pork belly
4 ounces (150 g) pitted black olives, divided
1 pound (500 g) duck breast
3 teaspoons salt
3 pinches freshly ground pepper
3 large eggs, divided
3 ¼ tablespoons heavy cream
1 ½ tablespoons unsalted butter, for greasing the mold
1 pound (500 g) shortcrust pastry (recipe p. 161)
2 ⅓ cups (550 g) aspic, at room temperature (recipe p. 171)

MAKES 6 SERVINGS

Using a knife, if necessary, debone the veal breast and chop it into approximately ¼-inch (7 mm) pieces (see Workshop, p. 21). Cut the chicken into ½-inch (1 ½-cm) cubes (see Workshop, p. 51).

Transfer the veal to a mixing bowl, add the salt and pepper, and mix by hand (see Workshop, p. 21) or with a mixer on low speed.

Add 1 egg and the cream and mix until uniform. Add the chicken. Vigorously mix by hand or in a mixer on low speed for 5 minutes. Refrigerate.

Grease the mold with the butter. Beat the remaining 2 eggs. Roll the dough to ⅛-inch (3-mm) thickness, cut it, and line the mold (see Workshop, p. 163). Add the filling. Seal the crust with the top piece of dough (see Workshop, p. 165). Cut 1 or 2 round holes in the top.

Place the mold in a cold oven. Set the temperature to 350°F (180°C) and bake using the convection setting (if possible) for 1 hour 10 minutes. Alternatively, monitor with a cooking thermometer and remove when the internal temperature reaches 145°F (64°C).

Allow it to rest for 30 minutes at room temperature, then refrigerate overnight. The next day, pour in the aspic as directed on p. 171. Chill for at least 1 hour before serving.

PREPARATION TIME
1 hour 45 minutes

COOKING TIME
1 hour 40 minutes

RESTING TIME
Overnight

PÂTÉS EN CROÛTE

LAMB PÂTÉ EN CROÛTE

◆ ◆ ◆

INGREDIENTS

1 head garlic
Olive oil, for brushing
1 pound (500 g) whole veal breast or 1 pound (500 g) minced veal breast
1 pound (500 g) boneless lamb shoulder, trimmed of fat
3 teaspoons salt
3 pinches freshly ground pepper
3 large eggs, divided
¼ cup (60 g) heavy cream
1 ½ tablespoons unsalted butter, for greasing the mold
1 pound (500 g) shortcrust pastry (recipe p. 161)
2 ⅓ cups (550 g) aspic, at room temperature (recipe p. 171)

MAKES 6 SERVINGS

Place the garlic in an oven-safe dish, generously brush with olive oil, and transfer to a cold oven. Set the temperature to 350°F (180 °C), and bake using the convection setting (if possible) for 30 minutes.

Using a knife, remove any bones from the veal breast. Chop the pork belly into approximately ¼-inch (7 mm) pieces (see Workshop, p. 21). Cut the lamb shoulder into ½-inch (1 ½-cm) cubes (see Workshop, p. 51). Peel the roasted garlic, halve the cloves, and remove the germ if needed.

In a mixing bowl, combine the veal breast and the salt and pepper. Mix either by hand (see Workshop, p. 21) or in a mixer on low speed.

Add 1 egg and the cream to the mixture, stirring until uniform. Add the lamb shoulder and garlic. Mix vigorously by hand or in a mixer on low speed for 5 minutes. Transfer to the refrigerator.

Grease the mold with the butter. Beat the remaining 2 eggs. Roll the dough to ⅛-inch (3-mm) thickness, cut it, and line the mold (see Workshop, p. 163). Add the filling. Seal the crust with the top piece of dough (see Workshop, p. 165). Cut 1 or 2 round holes in the top.

Place the mold in a cold oven. Set the temperature to 350°F (180°C) and bake using the convection setting (if possible) for 1 hour 10 minutes. Alternatively, monitor with a cooking thermometer and remove when the internal temperature reaches 145°F (64°C).

Allow it to rest for 30 minutes at room temperature, then refrigerate overnight. The next day, pour in the aspic as directed on p. 171. Chill for at least 1 hour before serving.

HANDMADE
IN SHEFFIELD

PREPARATION TIME
2 hours

COOKING TIME
2 hours 10 minutes

RESTING TIME
Overnight

OCTOPUS PÂTÉ EN CROÛTE

◆ ◆ ◆

INGREDIENTS

½ pound (250 g) octopus tentacles
1 lime, cut in half
¾ ounce (20 g) samphire (sea beans) or thin asparagus, chopped and divided
1 pound (500 g) whole pork belly or 1 pound (500 g) minced pork belly
¼ pound (150 g) boneless skinless chicken breast
2 teaspoons salt
2 pinches freshly ground pepper
3 large eggs, divided
¼ cup (60 g) heavy cream
1 ½ tablespoons unsalted butter, for greasing the mold
1 pound (500 g) shortcrust pastry (recipe p. 161)
2 ⅓ cups (550 g) aspic, at room temperature (recipe p. 171)

MAKES 6 SERVINGS

Bring a large pot of water to a boil and add the octopus, the juice from 1 lime half, and half the sea beans. Cook for approximately 1 hour. The octopus is ready when it can easily be pierced with a fork.

Using a knife, remove the rind and any bones from the pork belly, making sure to keep the fat on the belly (see Workshop, p. 21). Chop the pork belly into approximately ¼-inch (7 mm) pieces (see Workshop, p.21).

Cut the chicken into ½-inch (1 ½-cm) cubes. Cut the octopus tentacles into ½-inch (1 ½ cm) pieces (see Workshop, p. 51).

Zest the remaining half of the lime.

In a mixing bowl, combine the pork belly and the salt and pepper. Mix either by hand (see Workshop, p. 21) or in a mixer on low speed. Add 1 egg and the cream, and mix until uniform. Add the chicken, octopus, remaining sea beans, lime zest, and the juice from the remaining lime half. Mix vigorously by hand or with a mixer on low speed for 5 minutes. Transfer to the refrigerator.

Grease the mold with the butter. Beat the remaining 2 eggs. Roll the dough to ⅛-inch (3-mm) thickness, cut it, and line the mold (see Workshop, p. 163). Add the filling. Seal the crust with the top piece of dough (see Workshop, p. 165). Cut 1 or 2 round holes in the top.

Place the mold in a cold oven. Set the temperature to 350°F (180°C) and bake using the convection setting (if possible) for 1 hour 10 minutes. Alternatively, monitor with a cooking thermometer and remove when the internal temperature reaches 145°F (64°C).

Allow it to rest for 30 minutes at room temperature, then refrigerate overnight. The next day, pour in the aspic as directed on p. 171. Chill for at least 1 hour before serving.

PREPARATION TIME	COOKING TIME	RESTING TIME
1 day	1 hour 30 minutes	Overnight

PÂTÉS EN CROÛTE

PILLOW OF THE BEAUTIFUL DAWN

◆ ◆ ◆

INGREDIENTS

2 ¾ pounds (1 ¼ kg) whole pork belly or 2 ¼ pounds (1 kg) minced pork belly
3 ½ ounces (100 g) black truffles
2 ¾ pounds (1 ¼ kg) whole veal breast or 2 ¼ pounds (1 kg) ground veal breast
1 pound (500 g) boneless lean wild boar
1 pound (500 g) pheasant fillet
1 pound (500 g) boneless skinless chicken breast
1 pound (500 g) mallard duck fillet
1 pound (500 g) partridge fillet
4 ¼ tablespoons salt
2 teaspoons freshly ground pepper
7 large eggs, divided
1 cup (240 g) heavy cream, divided
½ cup (100 g) Armagnac, divided
3 ¼ pounds (1 ½ kg) shortcrust pastry (recipe p. 161)

MAKES 25 SERVINGS

Using a knife, remove the rind and any bones from the pork belly, making sure to keep the fat on the belly (see Workshop, p. 21). Chop the pork belly into approximately ¼-inch (7 mm) pieces (see Workshop, p. 21). Place in a mixing bowl.

Slice the truffle thinly and place in a bowl. Slice the veal breast thinly and place in another bowl. Cut the boar, pheasant, chicken, duck, and partridge lengthwise into strips approximately ¾ inch (2 cm) wide. Place each meat in a separate bowl.

Stir together the salt and pepper, then divide into three parts: the first being 50% of the total quantity and the remaining two 25% of the total quantity. Divide the 50% further into four parts and mix individually with the boar, pheasant, duck, and partridge.

Evenly distribute the remaining salt and pepper to season the pork belly and veal breast separately. Mix by hand (see Workshop, p. 21) or in a mixer on low speed.

Next add 2 eggs, ½ cup (100 g) of cream, and 2 ounces (50 g) of Armagnac to the bowl containing the pork belly. Mix until the mixture is uniform. Repeat the procedure with the bowl of veal.

Preheat the oven to 410°F (210°C), using the convection setting (if possible).

Roll out the dough to a ¼ -inch (7-mm) thickness, then divide into two parts for the bottom and top. The bottom dough should be large enough to fill a baking sheet without spilling over. The lid should be a third larger in both length and width than the base. Line the baking sheet with parchment paper and then lay the bottom dough on top.

This monumental French charcuterie recipe traces back to the early 19th century, conceived by the gastronome Brillat-Savarin in homage to his mother, who was named Aurore (Aurore is the French word for "dawn"). This grand pâté en croute was made from the finest game, veal, pork, foie gras, and truffles. This recipe is a more accessible rendition but remains a challenge for the bravest of connoisseurs!

Cover the bottom pastry with the veal belly, leaving a margin of about 1 ¼ inches (3 cm) of dough on all sides. Layer the truffles on top of the veal. Place all the strips of boar, duck, partridge, pheasant, and chicken lengthwise, alternating them. Cover everything with the pork belly.

Beat the remaining eggs. Brush a thin layer of the egg on the exposed edges of the dough. Place the top dough over the filling, ensuring it covers the contents snugly. Seal the edges where the egg was applied. Trim any excess pastry to ¾ inch (2 cm).

Apply slight pressure to ensure the edges are sealed and brush the "pillow" with the remaining egg. Make a round hole in the center of the top dough, approximately 1 ¼ inches (3 cm) in diameter.

Transfer the baking sheet to the oven and bake for 30 minutes. Reduce the temperature to 230°F (110°C) and bake for approximately 1 hour. The "pillow" is done when a cooking thermometer indicates the internal temperature has reached 145°F (64°C). Let it rest for 1 hour at room temperature, followed by a night in the refrigerator. Warm the slices in the oven before serving to accentuate the contrasting flavors.

PRESSED DISHES

STRAINING THE COOKING JUICE

Straining the cooking liquid allows the unique flavor of each ingredient to infuse the aspic.

USING A FINE-MESH STRAINER

This method is the most effective for straining due to the fine mesh of the chinois, especially when aided by a spatula for pressing down on the ingredients.

USING A CLOTH

STEP 1

An alternative approach involves lining a large bowl with a clean cloth and then adding the mixture to be strained.

STEP 2

Close and twist the cloth as if tying a knot, squeezing tightly to extract all the liquid.

UNMOLDING A PRESSED DISH

◆ ◆ ◆

Removing a pressed dish from its mold is a delicate yet crucial step to maintain its beautiful appearance. But if you follow the steps outlined below, unmolding will become simple.

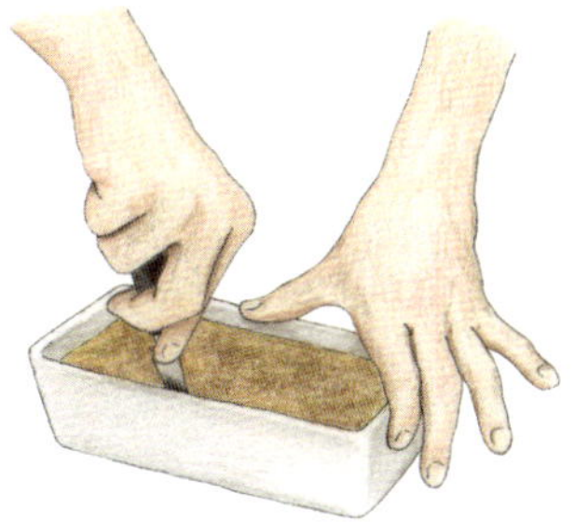

STEP 1

Run a sharp knife around all edges of the mold.

STEP 2

Fill a container with warm water. Immerse the mold three-quarters deep the water for about 10 seconds. This will loosen it from its base.

STEP 3

Gently flip over the mold onto a cutting board or presentation plate to release the terrine.

PREPARATION TIME	COOKING TIME	RESTING TIME
1 hour 45 minutes	4 hours	Overnight

PRESSED

PRESSED BEEF

◆ ◆ ◆

INGREDIENTS

2 small leeks
1 yellow onion
3 medium carrots, divided
2 ½ cups (600 ml) water
1 bunch parsley
2 garlic cloves, peeled
4 teaspoons salt
3 pinches freshly ground pepper
1 ¾ pounds (800 g) beef chuck
3 gelatin sheets or
1 ½ teaspoons powder

MAKES 6 SERVINGS

Trim the roots and green tops from the leeks, reserving the green tops. Coarsely chop the onion and cut 1 of the carrots into 6 pieces. In a large pot, bring the water to a boil. Add the parsley, garlic, onion, 1 of the carrots, the green tops of the leeks, and the salt and pepper. Reduce heat to low, and simmer for 30 minutes. Add the remaining 2 whole carrots, the leek whites, and the beef chuck, adding water if necessary to ensure all ingredients are covered.

Simmer, removing the whole carrots and leeks when they are fork-tender. Continue to simmer the beef until it is fork-tender, about 3 hours 30 minutes. Remove the beef from the broth and cool to room temperature.

Soak the gelatin sheets in cold water until the sheets have softened. Strain 2 ⅛ cups (600 ml) of the broth, and in a separate saucepan, bring it to a boil (see Workshop, p. 200). Taste the broth, adjust seasoning if necessary, and remove from heat.

Remove the gelatin sheets from the water, squeezing out any extra moisture, and whisk them into the hot broth. Set aside to cool to room temperature.

Hand-shred the beef (see Workshop, p. 109).

Quarter the carrots and leeks lengthwise. Fill a mold one-third full with beef, and pour in enough aspic to level it. Top with half of the carrots and half the leeks, alternating them. Continue layering beef and vegetables as described, ending with beef on top and then another pour of aspic.

Allow the terrine to rest for 30 minutes at room temperature. Cover with plastic wrap and refrigerate overnight. Unmold before serving (see Workshop, p. 201).

PREPARATION TIME	COOKING TIME	RESTING TIME
1 hour 45 minutes	2 hours 30 minutes	Overnight

PRESSED

PRESSED GARRIGUE HERBED RABBIT

◆ ◆ ◆

INGREDIENTS

2 ½ cups (600 ml) water
1 yellow onion
1 bunch parsley, divided
2 garlic cloves, peeled
1 onion
3 teaspoons salt
3 pinches freshly ground pepper
2 medium carrots
1 medium zucchini
2 ¾ pounds (1 ½ kg) rabbit legs
3 gelatin sheets or
1 ½ teaspoons powder

MAKES 5 SERVINGS

In a large pot, bring the water to a boil. Coarsely chop the onion. Add ⅔ of the parsley leaves and the garlic, onion, and salt and pepper. Reduce heat to low, and simmer for 30 minutes.

While the mixture simmers, trim and peel the carrots and zucchini. Mince the remaining ⅓ bunch parsley leaves and set aside.

After 30 minutes, add the carrots, zucchini, and rabbit to the pot, adding water if necessary to ensure all ingredients are covered. Simmer, removing the whole carrots and zucchini when they are fork-tender. Continue to simmer the rabbit until it is fork-tender, about 2 hours. Remove the rabbit from the broth and cool to room temperature.

Soak the gelatin sheets in cold water until the sheets have softened. Strain 2 ⅛ cups (500 ml) of the cooking broth, and in a separate saucepan, bring it to a boil (see Workshop, p. 200). Taste the broth, adjust seasoning if necessary, and remove from heat.

Remove the gelatin sheets from the water, squeezing out any extra moisture, and whisk them into the hot broth. Set aside to cool to room temperature.

Shred the rabbit by hand, retaining only the meat (see Workshop, p.109).

Quarter the carrots lengthwise and cut the zucchini into eighths lengthwise. Mix the chopped parsley into the aspic. Fill a mold one-third full with the rabbit, and pour in enough aspic to level it. Top with half the carrots and half the zucchini, alternating them. Continue layering rabbit and vegetables as described, ending with rabbit on top and then another pour of aspic.

Allow the terrine to rest for 30 minutes at room temperature. Cover with plastic wrap and refrigerate overnight. Unmold before serving (see Workshop, p. 201).

PREPARATION TIME
1 hour 30 minutes

COOKING TIME
2 hours 30 minutes

RESTING TIME
Overnight

PRESSED CHICKEN WITH CANDIED LEMON

◆ ◆ ◆

INGREDIENTS

10 ½ cups (600 ml) water
1 medium carrot
1 yellow onion
1 bunch parsley
2 garlic cloves, peeled
3 teaspoons plus 1 pinch salt
4 pinches freshly ground pepper
2 ¾ pounds (1 ¼ kg) bone-in chicken thighs
2 lemons
1 cup (200 g) granulated sugar
1 medium zucchini
Olive oil, for drizzling
3 gelatin sheets or 1 ½ teaspoons powder

MAKES 5 SERVINGS

In a large pot, bring 10 ½ cups (600 ml) of the water to a boil. Cut the carrot into 6 pieces and coarsely chop the onion. To the pot, add the carrot, onion, parsley, garlic, 3 teaspoons of the salt, and 3 pinches of the pepper. Reduce heat to low, and simmer for 30 minutes. Add the chicken, adding water if necessary to ensure all ingredients are covered. Simmer the chicken until it is fork-tender, about 2 hours. Remove the chicken and cool to room temperature.

While chicken cooks, cut the lemons into ⅓-inch (1-cm) slices. In a medium pot, bring 1 cup (240 ml) water to a boil, stir in the sugar, and reduce to medium heat. Add half the lemon slices and let them simmer for 15 minutes. Remove the lemons from the pot with a slotted spoon and set aside to cool. Repeat with the remaining lemon slices.

Preheat the oven to 320°F (160°C). Slice the zucchini lengthwise into eight pieces. Transfer to a baking sheet, drizzle with olive oil and season with the remaining 1 pinch each of the salt and pepper, and bake for 1 hour.

Soak the gelatin sheets in cold water until the sheets have softened. Strain 2 ⅛ cups (500 g) of the cooking broth, and in a separate saucepan, bring it to a boil (see Workshop, p. 200). Taste the broth, adjust seasoning if necessary, and remove from heat. Remove the gelatin sheets from the water, squeezing out any extra moisture, and whisk them into the hot broth. Set aside to cool to room temperature.Shred the chicken by hand (see Workshop, p. 109), retaining only the meat. Layer the bottom of a mold with lemon slices. Then fill the mold one-third full with the chicken, and pour in enough aspic to level it. Repeat with another layer of lemon, chicken, and aspic. Then add the zucchini in a layer, and end with chicken on top and then another pour of aspic.

Allow the terrine to rest for 30 minutes at room temperature. Cover with plastic wrap and refrigerate overnight. Unmold before serving (see Workshop, p. 201).

PREPARATION TIME
1 hour 45 minutes

COOKING TIME
2 hours 30 minutes

RESTING TIME
Overnight

PRESSED SUNLIT VEGETABLES

◆ ◆ ◆

INGREDIENTS

1 medium carrot
1 yellow onion
1 bunch parsley
2 garlic cloves, peeled
3 teaspoons plus 2 pinches salt
5 pinches freshly ground pepper
2 large artichokes
3 green or yellow bell peppers
3 medium tomatoes
2 medium zucchini
Olive oil, for drizzling
3 gelatin sheets or
1 ½ teaspoons powder
4 ¼ cups (1 l) water

MAKES 6 SERVINGS

In a large pot, bring the water to a boil. Cut the carrot into 6 pieces and coarsely chop the onion. Add the carrot, onion, parsley, garlic, 3 teaspoons of salt, and 3 pinches of pepper. Reduce heat to low, and simmer for 1 hour. Fill another large pot with salted water, bring to a boil, and add the artichokes and boil for 30 minutes. Remove artichokes and set aside to cool.

Quarter the bell peppers, removing the seeds and membranes. Quarter the tomatoes, removing the stems and juice, keeping only the flesh. Slice the zucchini lengthwise into eight pieces. Place peppers, tomatoes, and zucchini on a baking sheet. Drizzle with olive oil and season with 1 pinch each of salt and pepper. Bake in oven set to 320°F (160°C). Remove the tomatoes after 15 minutes and continue cooking the bell peppers and zucchini for another 45 minutes. Cool, then peel the skins from the tomatoes and bell peppers.

Soak the gelatin sheets in cold water until the sheets have softened. Strain 2 ⅛ cups (500 g) of cooking broth, and in a separate saucepan, bring it to a boil (see Workshop, p. 200). Remove from heat. Remove the gelatin sheets from the water, squeezing out any extra moisture, and whisk them into the hot broth. Set aside to cool to room temperature.

Remove all the leaves from the artichokes and discard the choke. Slice the artichoke stems in half. Layer the bottom of a mold with bell peppers, and pour in enough aspic to level it. Sprinkle with 1 pinch each of the salt and pepper. Layer the zucchini next, followed by another pour of aspic. Layer the tomatoes, then the artichokes. Repeat the process in the same order for all ingredients ending with a layer of aspic on top. Allow the terrine to rest for 30 minutes at room temperature. Cover with plastic wrap and refrigerate overnight. Unmold before serving (see Workshop, p. 201).

HERBS

A TOUCH OF LIGHTNESS

◆ ◆ ◆

Whether raw or cooked, herbs, with their rich aromatic profiles, elevate dishes. They lend character to pâtés, elegance to terrines, freshness to pâtés en croûte, uniqueness to rillettes, and vibrancy to pressed dishes. However, it's vital to use them in a manner suited to each specific recipe.

WHICH HERB FOR WHAT PURPOSE?

PARSLEY

Parsley is undeniably a favorite among makers of charcuterie, gracing numerous regional specialties like parsley-infused ham. It imparts a refreshing essence to dishes, whether baked in a terrine or served raw in a pressed dish.

TARRAGON

With its bright flavor, tarragon demands attention and enhances dishes with its zest. Use it sparingly, however, to avoid overshadowing other flavors.

THYME AND BAY LEAF

Thyme and bay leaf are ingredients in the quintessential bouquet garni, ideal for accompanying broth. Their robustness brings a touch of Provence to your charcuterie.

CHERVIL

Visually, chervil might seem like parsley's younger sibling, but it stands out with its faintly aniseed flavor. It can be used similarly to parsley.

CILANTRO

People either love or loathe the spicy, pungent, and citrusy notes of cilantro. To preserve its flavors, it's best to coarsely chop and add it toward the end, without cooking.

BASIL

The potent aroma of basil shines brightest when uncooked. Hence, it's best added at the last moment, coarsely chopped—perfect for a modern twist on rillettes.

PREPARATION TIME
1 hour 30 minutes

COOKING TIME
2 hours 30 minutes

RESTING TIME
Overnight

PRESSED

PRESSED HERB-INFUSED CHICKEN

◆ ◆ ◆

INGREDIENTS

12 ¾ cups (3 l) water
1 yellow onion
2 bunches parsley, divided
2 garlic cloves, peeled
2 teaspoons salt
2 pinches freshly ground pepper
1 bunch tarragon
1 bunch cilantro
3 ½ pounds (1 ½ kg) bone-in chicken thighs
3 gelatin sheets or 1 ½ teaspoons powder

MAKES 6 SERVINGS

In a large pot, bring the water to a boil. Coarsely chop the onion and add it to the pot, along with 1 bunch of the parsley, the garlic, and the salt and pepper. Reduce heat to low, and simmer for 30 minutes.

Add the chicken, adding water if necessary to ensure all ingredients are covered. Simmer the chicken until it is fork-tender, about 2 hours. Remove the chicken and cool to room temperature.

While the chicken cooks, mince the tarragon, cilantro, and the remaining parsley leaves.

Soak the gelatin sheets in cold water until the sheets have softened. Strain 2 ⅛ cups (500 ml) of the cooking broth, and in a separate saucepan, bring it to a boil (see Workshop, p. 200). Taste the broth, adjust seasoning if necessary, and remove from heat.

Remove the gelatin sheets from the water, squeezing out any extra moisture, and whisk them into the hot broth. Set aside to cool to room temperature.

Shred the cooked chicken by hand, retaining only the meat (see Workshop, p. 109). In a large bowl, mix the finely chopped herbs and chicken with the aspic.

Fill a mold with the chicken-herb-broth mixture.

Allow the terrine to rest for 30 minutes at room temperature. Cover with plastic wrap and refrigerate overnight. Unmold before serving (see Workshop, p. 201).

PREPARATION TIME
1 hour 30 minutes

COOKING TIME
2 hours 30 minutes

RESTING TIME
Overnight

PRESSED WHOLE CHICKEN

◆ ◆ ◆

INGREDIENTS

10 ½ cups (2 ½ l) water
1 yellow onion
1 medium carrot
1 bunch parsley
2 garlic cloves, peeled
4 teaspoons salt
3 pinches freshly ground pepper
3 shallots
2 ¾ pounds (1.2 kg) bone-in chicken thighs
5 ¼ ounces (150 g) boneless skinless chicken breast
3 ½ ounces (100 g) pistachios
3 gelatin sheets or 1 ½ teaspoons powder

MAKES 6 SERVINGS

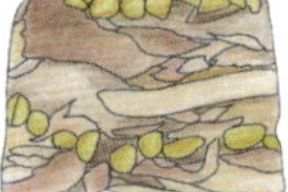

In a large pot, bring the water to a boil. Coarsely chop the onion and cut the carrot into 6 pieces. Add them to the pot, along with the parsley, garlic, and the salt and pepper. Reduce heat to low, and simmer for 30 minutes.

Without peeling them, place the shallots on a baking sheet and transfer to a cold oven. Set the oven to 320°F (160°C) and bake for 30 minutes. Let shallots cool, then peel and halve them.

Add the chicken thighs and breast to the pot, adding water if necessary to ensure all ingredients are covered. Simmer the chicken until it is fork-tender, about 2 hours. Remove the chicken and cool to room temperature.

Soak the gelatin sheets in cold water until the sheets have softened. Strain 2 ⅛ cups (500 ml) of the cooking broth, and in a separate saucepan, bring it to a boil (see Workshop, p. 200). Taste the broth, adjust seasoning if necessary, and remove from heat.

Remove the gelatin sheets from the water, squeezing out any extra moisture, and whisk them into the hot broth. Set aside to cool to room temperature.

Shred the cooked chicken by hand, retaining only the meat (see Workshop, p. 109). Fill a mold one-third full with shredded chicken, and pour in enough aspic to level it. Add a layer of shallots and pistachios and cover with more aspic. Continue layering in this manner until the mold is filled, finishing with a layer of aspic on top.

Allow the terrine to rest for 30 minutes at room temperature. Cover with plastic wrap and refrigerate overnight. Unmold before serving (see Workshop, p. 201).

PRADEL

PREPARATION TIME
1 hour 30 minutes

COOKING TIME
3 hours

RESTING TIME
Overnight

PRESSED DUCK WITH CANDIED ORANGES

◆ ◆ ◆

INGREDIENTS

12 cups (3 l) plus 1 ¼ cups (300 ml) water
1 yellow onion
1 carrot
1 bunch parsley
2 garlic cloves, peeled
4 teaspoons salt
4 pinches freshly ground pepper
1 ¾ pounds (800 g) raw duck thighs
2 oranges
1 ½ cups (300 g) granulated sugar
2 gelatin sheets or 1 teaspoons powder

MAKES 6 SERVINGS

In a large pot, bring 12 cups (3 l) of the water to a boil. Coarsely chop the onion, cut the carrot into 6 pieces, and add them to the pot, along with the parsley, garlic, and the salt and pepper. Reduce heat to low, and simmer for 30 minutes.

Add the duck thighs to the pot, adding water if necessary to ensure all ingredients are covered. Simmer the duck until it is fork-tender and beginning to pull away from the bone, about 2 hours 30 minutes. Remove the duck and cool to room temperature.

Cut the oranges into ⅓-inch (1-cm) slices. In a medium pot over medium heat, combine the remaining 1 ¼ cups (300 ml) of water with the sugar. Stir until the sugar dissolves. Add the orange slices, reduce the heat to low, and simmer for 1 hour.

Soak the gelatin sheets in cold water until the sheets have softened. Strain 2 ⅛ cups (500 ml) of the cooking broth, and in a separate saucepan, bring it to a boil (see Workshop, p. 200). Taste the broth, adjust seasoning if necessary, and remove from heat.

Remove the gelatin sheets from the water, squeezing out any extra moisture, and whisk them into the hot broth. Set aside to cool to room temperature.

Shred the duck by hand, retaining only the meat (see Workshop, p. 109). Line the bottom of a mold with the orange slices. Fill the mold one-quarter full with shredded duck, and pour in enough aspic to level it. Top with a layer of orange slices. Continue with another layer of shredded duck and aspic. Add another layer of orange slices. Finish by adding the remaining shredded duck and a pour of aspic.

Allow the terrine to rest for 30 minutes at room temperature. Cover with plastic wrap and refrigerate overnight. Unmold before serving (see Workshop, p. 201).

PREPARATION TIME
1 hour 30 minutes

COOKING TIME
2 hours 30 minutes

RESTING TIME
Overnight

PRESSED WINTER VEGETABLES

◆ ◆ ◆

INGREDIENTS

6 cups (1 ½ l) water
14 ounces (400 g) small leeks
1 yellow onion
1 medium carrot
1 bunch parsley
2 garlic cloves, peeled
3 teaspoons salt
3 pinches freshly ground pepper
14 ounces (400 g) pumpkin
7 ounces (200 g) Brussels sprouts
10 ½ ounces (300 g) white button mushrooms
3 gelatin sheets or
1 ½ teaspoons powder

MAKES 6 SERVINGS

Trim the roots and green tops from the leeks, reserving the green tops. Coarsely chop the onion and cut the carrot into 6 pieces. In a large pot, bring the water to a boil. Add the green tops of the leeks, the onion, carrot, parsley, garlic, and the salt and pepper. Reduce heat to low, and simmer for 30 minutes.

While the broth cooks, peel the pumpkin and remove the seeds, and cut the flesh into ⅓-inch (1-cm) slices. Trim the Brussels sprouts and the mushrooms.

Add the pumpkin, Brussels sprouts, mushrooms, and white part of the leeks to the pot. Simmer, removing each ingredient when it is fork-tender. Let the vegetables cool to room temperature.

Soak the gelatin sheets in cold water until the sheets have softened. Strain 2 ⅛ cups (500 ml) of the cooking broth, and in a separate saucepan, bring it to a boil (see Workshop, p. 200). Taste the broth, adjust seasoning if necessary, and remove from heat.

Remove the gelatin sheets from the water, squeezing out any extra moisture, and whisk them into the hot broth. Set aside to cool to room temperature.

Separate the mushroom caps and stems. Chop the stems. Halve the Brussels sprouts.

Layer the bottom of a mold with the Brussels sprouts, then leeks, pumpkin, and mushrooms. Pour in enough aspic to level it. Place the remaining Brussels sprouts with their rounded side facing the interior of the terrine and cover with aspic. Follow with the remaining pumpkin, then aspic, then the remaining leeks and more aspic. Position the mushroom caps with their rounded side facing outward, fill the gaps with chopped mushrooms, and pour aspic to cover.

Allow the terrine to rest for 30 minutes at room temperature. Cover with plastic wrap and refrigerate overnight. Unmold before serving (see Workshop, p. 201).

PREPARATION TIME	COOKING TIME	RESTING TIME
1 hour 45 minutes	2 hours 30 minutes	Overnight

PRESSED

PRESSED COLORFUL CHICKEN

◆ ◆ ◆

INGREDIENTS

1 yellow onion
3 medium carrots, divided
10 ½ cups (2 ½ l) water
1 bunch parsley
2 garlic cloves, peeled
4 teaspoons salt
3 pinches freshly ground pepper
2 ¼ pounds (1 kg) bone-in chicken thighs
2 red beets
3 gelatin sheets or 1 ½ teaspoons powder

MAKES 6 SERVINGS

Coarsely chop the onion and cut 1 carrot into 6 pieces. In a large pot, bring the water to a boil. Add the onion and carrot, and the parsley, garlic, salt, and pepper. Reduce heat to low, and simmer for 30 minutes.

Add the chicken thighs, beets, and remaining 2 carrots to the pot, adding water if necessary to ensure all ingredients are covered. Simmer, removing the beets and carrots when they are fork-tender. Let the vegetables cool to room temperature. Simmer the chicken until it is fork-tender and the meat easily pulls away from the bone, about 2 hours. Remove the chicken and cool to room temperature.

Soak the gelatin sheets in cold water until the sheets have softened. Strain 2 ⅛ cups (500 ml) of the cooking broth, and in a separate saucepan, bring it to a boil (see Workshop, p. 200). Taste the broth, adjust seasoning if necessary, and remove from heat.

Remove the gelatin sheets from the water, squeezing out any extra moisture, and whisk them into the hot broth. Set aside to cool to room temperature.

Peel the beets and cut into ⅓-inch (1-cm) slices. Quarter the carrots lengthwise.

Shred the chicken by hand, retaining only the meat (see Workshop, p. 109).

Layer the bottom of a mold with beet slices. Fill the mold one-third full with shredded chicken, and pour in enough aspic to level it. Add a layer of carrot slices and add more chicken until the mold is two-thirds full. Pour in more aspic to level it. Finish with the remaining beet slices, then add the remaining chicken, and pour aspic to level it.

Allow the terrine to rest for 30 minutes at room temperature. Cover with plastic wrap and refrigerate overnight. Unmold before serving (see Workshop, p. 201).

PREPARATION TIME
1 hour 30 minutes

COOKING TIME
3 hours

RESTING TIME
Overnight

PRESSED

PRESSED LAMB, ALMONDS & APPLE

◆◆◆

INGREDIENTS

1 yellow onion
1 medium carrot
10 ½ cups (2 ½ l) water
1 bunch parsley
2 garlic cloves, peeled
3 teaspoons salt
3 pinches freshly ground pepper
2 medium apples
3 ½ ounces (100 g) almonds
1 ½ tablespoons unsalted butter
3 tablespoons granulated sugar
1 ¾ pounds (800 g) boneless lamb shoulder
3 gelatin sheets or
1 ½ teaspoons powder

MAKES 6 SERVINGS

Coarsely chop the onion and cut the carrot into 6 pieces. In a large pot, bring the water to a boil. Add the onion and carrot, and the parsley, garlic, salt, and pepper. Reduce heat to low, and simmer for 30 minutes. While the broth simmers, peel, core, and quarter the apples. Cut each quarter in half lengthwise. In a medium skillet over high heat, toast the almonds for 2 minutes, stirring constantly. Remove the almonds from the skillet and set aside to cool. In the same skillet, over medium heat, melt the butter and sauté the apple pieces for 2 minutes. Add the sugar and continue stirring until the apples are soft and slightly colored. Remove from heat and cool to room temperature.

Add the lamb to the pot, adding water if necessary to ensure all ingredients are covered. Simmer the lamb until it is fork-tender, about 1 hour 30 minutes. Remove the lamb and cool to room temperature.

Soak the gelatin sheets in cold water until the sheets have softened. Strain 2 ⅛ cups (500 ml) of the cooking broth, and in a separate saucepan, bring it to a boil (see Workshop, p. 200). Taste the broth, adjust seasoning if necessary, and remove from heat. Remove the gelatin sheets from the water, squeezing out any extra moisture, and whisk them into the hot broth. Set aside to cool to room temperature.

Shred the lamb by hand, retaining only the meat (see Workshop, p. 109). Fill a mold one-third full with lamb, then pour in aspic to level. Add the apple pieces. Next, add another layer of lamb until two-thirds full, then pour in aspic to level. Add a layer of toasted almonds. Finish with a final layer of lamb and pour in aspic to level.

Allow the terrine to rest for 30 minutes at room temperature. Cover with plastic wrap and refrigerate overnight. Unmold before serving (see Workshop, p. 201).

PREPARATION TIME
1 hour 30 minutes

COOKING TIME
2 hours 30 minutes

RESTING TIME
Overnight

PRESSED

PRESSED RABBIT, TOMATOES & OLIVE

◆ ◆ ◆

INGREDIENTS

1 yellow onion
1 medium carrot
10 ½ cups (2 ½ l) water
1 bunch parsley
2 garlic cloves, peeled
4 teaspoons plus 1 pinch salt
4 pinches freshly ground pepper
5 medium tomatoes
Olive oil, for drizzling
5 ¼ ounces (150 g) pitted olives
2 ¾ pounds (1 ¼ kg) rabbit thighs
3 gelatin sheets or
1 ½ teaspoons powder

MAKES 6 SERVINGS

Coarsely chop the onion and cut the carrot into 6 pieces. In a large pot, bring the water to a boil. Add the onion and carrot, and the parsley, garlic, 4 teaspoons of the salt, and 3 pinches of the pepper. Reduce heat to low, and simmer for 30 minutes. While the broth simmers, stem and core the tomatoes, reserving the juice. Quarter the tomatoes, and add any additional tomato juice to the simmering broth. Place tomatoes on an baking sheet, drizzle with olive oil, and season with 1 pinch each of the salt and pepper. Place in a cold oven set to 300°F (150°C) for 15 minutes. Let tomatoes cool and then peel the skins off. Cut the olives in half and set aside.

Add the rabbit thighs to the pot, adding water if necessary to ensure all ingredients are covered. Simmer the rabbit until it is fork-tender, about 2 hours. Remove the rabbit and cool to room temperature.

Soak the gelatin sheets in cold water until the sheets have softened. Strain 2 ⅛ cups (500 ml) of the cooking broth, and in a separate saucepan, bring it to a boil (see Workshop, p. 200). Taste the broth, adjust seasoning if necessary, and remove from heat. Remove the gelatin sheets from the water, squeezing out any extra moisture, and whisk them into the hot broth. Set aside to cool to room temperature.

Shred the rabbit by hand, retaining only the meat (see Workshop, p. 109). Fill a mold one-quarter full with rabbit, then pour in aspic to level. Add half the tomatoes lengthwise. Cover with rabbit until half-full, then pour in aspic to level. Add a layer of olives and cover with aspic. Add more rabbit until three-quarters full, then pour in aspic to level. Add the remaining tomatoes. Finish with the remaining rabbit and pour in aspic to level.

Allow the terrine to rest for 30 minutes at room temperature. Cover with plastic wrap and refrigerate overnight. Unmold before serving (see Workshop, p. 201).

RECIPES

TABLES

RECIPES

LESSON IN HOMEMADE CHARCUTERIE

INDEX

ACKNOWLEDGMENTS

Thank you to the entire team at Maison Verot
for continually raising the standard of charcuterie.

◆

A heartfelt thank you to Emmanuel Le Vallois, who welcomed
this project with enthusiasm from our first meeting.

◆

Gratitude to Hélène Sevin, Aude Le Pichon, Sabine Houplain, and Benoit Berger,
as well as the outstanding team at Éditions du Chêne.

◆

Our appreciation goes to David Japy, with whom we shared
many moments of camaraderie during the photographing of the recipes.

◆

A special mention to Éliane Cheung, whose talented hand added
softness and elegance to our charcuterie illustrations.

◆

Thank you to the charcutiers-for-a-day who took the time to test a recipe
and provide us with invaluable feedback.

Christine Legeret and David Japy extend their thanks to:
Le Creuset (www.lecreuset.fr) - La Trésorerie (www.latresorerie.fr) - Maison Empereur (www.empereur.fr)
Peugeot (www.peugeot-saveurs.com) - Perceval (www.couteau.com) - Staub (www.zwilling.com/fr/staub).

French Charcuterie at Home: Terrines, Rillettes, Saucisses & Pâtés en Croûte was first published in the United States by Tra Publishing in 2024.

First published in 2020 by Éditions du Chêne–Hachette Livre
www.editionsduchene.fr

U.S. EDITION TEAM
Publisher and Creative Director: Ilona Oppenheim
Art Director: Jefferson Quintana
Editorial Director: Lisa McGuinness
Publishing Coordinator: Jessica Faroy
Typesetter: Morgane Leoni

FRENCH EDITION TEAM
Director: Emmanuel Le Vallois
Artistic Direction: Sabine Houplain
Typography and Design: Bureau Berger
Publishing: Hélène Sevin assisted by Aude Le Pichon
Styling: Christine Legeret
Production: Rémy Chauvière
Photogravure: Chromostyle

This book is printed on Forest Stewardship Council®-certified paper from supporting responsible forestry.

Tra Publishing is committed to sustainability
in its materials and practices.

Printed and bound in China by Artron Art Co., Ltd.

ISBN: 978-1-962098-07-6

Tra Publishing
245 NE 37th Street
Miami, FL 33137
trapublishing.com

1 2 3 4 5 6 7 8 9 10

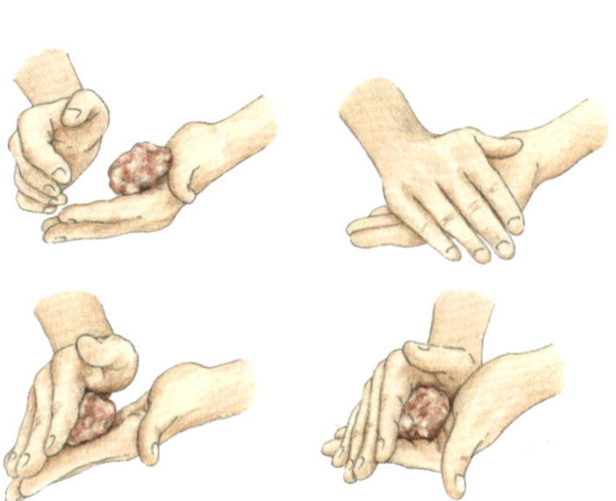

This book focuses on seasonality, highlights the true art of charcuterie and introduces soulful French cooking into your home.

—**DANIEL BOULUD**

THE DEFINITIVE GUIDE TO FRENCH CHARCUTERIE

The renowned Maison Verot in Paris presents 89 accessible recipes crafted by father and son charcutiers, Gilles and Nicolas Verot. Detailed line drawings illustrate step-by-step techniques to master the art of charcuterie, and beautiful photographs provide a visual reference for each dish. From the fine art of dicing, shredding, and layering to the creation of delicious pâtés, terrines, rillettes, and more, this ode to French charcuterie will delight both taste buds and eyes.

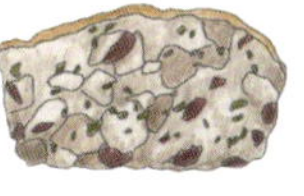

PÂTÉ

TERRINE

RILLETTES

PRESSED DISH

PÂTÉ EN CROÛTE

PIES & TORTES

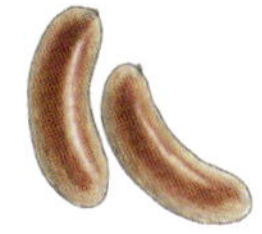

SAUSAGE

$45.00 US / $60.00 CAN
ISBN 978-1-962098-07-6

tra.publishing